Changing Cities, Shifting Stages

Previously Published Books by Blair A. Ruble

Soviet Trade Unions
Leningrad
Money Sings
Second Metropolis
Creating Diversity Capital
Washington's U Street
The Muse of Urban Delirium
Proclaiming Presence from the Washington Stage
The Arts of War

Changing Cities, Shifting Stages

How the Performing Arts Reveal Urban Transformation

Blair A. Ruble

Washington, DC

Copyright © 2024 by Blair A. Ruble

New Academia Publishing, 2024

All rights reserved. No part of this book may be reproduced or transmitted in any form or by any means, electronic or mechanical, including photocopying, recording, or by any information storage and retrieval system.

Printed in the United States of America

Library of Congress Control Number: 2024922448
ISBN 979-8-9900542-9-5 paperback (alk. paper)

New Academia Publishing, 4401-A Connecticut Ave. NW, #236,
Washington, DC 20008
info@newacademia.com - www.newacademia.com

For Grandmother Gertie and Aunt Mimi,
whose tales of early twentieth century New York opera,
theater, and music filled me with a love of cities and the arts
that has lasted a lifetime.

Contents

Acknowledgments	ix
1 Introduction: Changing Cities, Shifting Stages	1
2 Montreal: Moving Center Stage—Dance and Modernization in the Late Twentieth Century	17
3 Washington: Experimental Theater in Community Service—The Theater Club Engages Race Relations	37
4 Toronto in the 1970s as 1920s Paris: Imagining a National Identity from the Stage	53
5 Kyiv in the Twenty-First Century: From Provincial City to International Capital	75
6 Nashville: Music Makes the Town—The Growth of Country Music and the City's Rise	99
7 Concluding Observations	115
About the Author	120
Notes	121
Index	142

Acknowledgements

This volume brings together several lines of inquiry that began years, even decades, ago. As I have pursued them, I have realized that many seemingly disparate storylines play off one another, as I have attempted to work through the interrelationship between the arts and urban life. I would need a second volume as large as this one to thank all the colleagues who have helped me along my way.

I obviously am not able to offer thanks to all these people. I only hope that some will recognize themselves in what I have written. I can, however, mention colleagues who have helped me work through the preparation of this manuscript in myriad important ways. Thank you, Kengo Akizuki, Philip Arnoult, Marjorie Mandelstam Balzer, Harley Balzer, Cristina Bejan, Gerald Easer, Derek Hyra, Maurice Jackson, Mikhail Minakov, Natalia Moussienko, Andryi Puchkov, Yaroslav Pylynskyi, Izabella Tabarovsky, John Stanley, as well as two thoughtful anonymous reviewers. Master editor Alfred F. Imhoff has helped the manuscript immeasurably, as is his wont. I very much appreciate indexer Enid Zafran's invaluable assistance as well. Anna Lawton and her team with New Academia Press have proven themselves to be wonderful colleagues once again.

I would like to make special mention of the assistance provided by Janet Spikes, Librarian, and the magnificent staff at the Wilson Center Library, as well as by Leah Richardson, Special Collections Librarian, and the staff of the Special Collections Research Center at The George Washington University's Gelman Library. All researchers know that professional librarians are among our most essential colleagues.

Earlier versions of portions of this text have appeared as:

"Moving Center Stage: Dance and Modernization in Late-Twentieth-Century Montreal, *Suchasne mistetstvo* [Kyiv], 2018, no. 14: 69–82.
"How Toronto Became Toronto," in *Sotsial'naia antropologiia goroda*, ed. E. A. Okladnikova (Saint Petersburg: PGPU in A. I. Gertsena, 2018), 45–56.
"Riotous Performances," *Khudozhnia kul'tura: Aktual'nyi problem / Artistic Culture: Topical Issues* (Kyiv: Modern Art Research Institute) 17, no. 1 (2021): 17–29.
"Experimental Theater in Community Service: A History of the Washington Theater Club, 1957–1974," *American University Metropolitan Policy Center Working Papers*, Washington, March 2023.
Wilson Center, Kennan Institute's *Ukrainian Focus Blog: The Arts of War*, March 2022–present.
The Arts of War: Ukrainian Artists Confront Russia: Year One & Year Two (Stuttgart: Ibidem Verlag, 2023 & 2024).

Blair A. Ruble
Washington, DC
September 2024

Chapter 1

Introduction: Changing Cities, Shifting Stages

Prologue

France, especially Paris, was in the throes of deep generational division as the 1820s drew to a close. The generation that had come of age under the Old Regime embraced traditional understandings of how society, in all its aspects, should function—with a hefty measure of form over substance, predictability over innovation, hierarchy over parity, and order over disarray. The elderly Charles X, the younger brother of King Louis XVI and King Louis XVIII, personified the Bourbon Restoration imposed by the victorious powers meeting in Vienna to construct Europe's post-Napoleonic settlement. Those who had come of age after the 1789 Revolution—and during Napoleon's rule—embraced the slogans of their era praising Liberty, Equality, and Fraternity. They stood in stark opposition to all that the restored monarchy represented.

These political, social, and economic divisions found expression in the arts as "Classicists" defending the Old Regime's values faced off against a younger generation of "Romanticists" demanding a transformation to meet new realities. Romanticism—which favored individual expression, sentiment, and the heroic deeds of great people and historic epochs—had emerged in Germany and England during the last decades of the eighteenth century. The movement arrived in France early in the nineteenth century, where it became entwined with countless widening societal divisions in the wake of the Revolution and the rise of Napoleon.

By the mid-1820s, "Romantics" were striving to recreate every art form in their image. Their efforts generated bitter conflicts in nearly every French cultural and educational institution. The Romantics produced a distinctive lifestyle of informality and indecorous behavior—an early model for the American Counterculturalists of the 1960s—that deeply offended their elders. As the march of generational change swept through France's highly institutionalized artistic scene, the Old Royalists fought back. In the process, the Romantics discovered a wizard of their own: Victor Hugo.[1]

Hugo was an odd idol for rebellious youth. The son of a general in Napoleon's army, he was well connected among the country's most powerful families. Indeed, he was the official poet at the 1825 Coronation of Charles X in Rheims. Furthermore, Hugo had been named a *chevalier* of the Légion d'Honneur. Aesthetically, however, he was proving to be a soul mate of his generation's Romanticists.

Highly ambitious, Hugo deeply coveted a place in the prestigious Académie Française representing the legendary "forty immortals" of French language and literature. Being denied more than once—the academy elected him as a member only in 1841—he set out to storm the traditionalists' ramparts. He began writing pathbreaking novels, such as *Le Dernier jour d'un condamné* (*The Last Day of a Condemned Man*), which charted a new path to what would become a modern focus on the internal lives of literary protagonists. By the late 1820s, he agreed to an invitation from Baron Taylor, the freshly appointed director of the Comédie Française, to write a play to be performed at the company's elegant new home, the Théâtre de l'Odéon, next to the Luxembourg Gardens.

Dating from 1680, the Comédie Française preserved the traditionalist Classicist dramaturgy of the Old Regime. Royalists filled the company's audiences resisting newfangled notions of modernity. Hugo, perhaps inevitably, encountered opposition from the regime's censors when he presented his first effort—a five-act play *Un Duel sous Richelieu* (later retitled *Marion de Larme*) in June 1829.

Initially, the theater's reading committee accepted the play. The censors, however, balked at Act IV, which portrayed a dawdling Louis XIII reigning over his realm's decline. Once the censors took issue, Hugo turned to Minister of the Interior Martignac to overrule his subordinate's decision. Martignac feared that theater audiences would view the portrayal of Louis XIII as a thinly vailed slap at King Charles. Losing once again, Hugo turned to the king himself. By mid-August, Charles similarly vetoed the proposed performance (though he offered Hugo a state pension as recompense). Hugo shared these exchanges with the public, firing up the young Romanticists in protest over censorship.

Rather than revise his first play, Hugo wrote another: *Hernani, ou l'Honneur Castillan*. The story is of a beautiful Castilian maiden who is subjected to the unwanted advances of a repulsive old man. Hugo's verse drew on idiomatic—even provocative—language of the day to move the action inevitably to the joint suicide of Doña Sol and her lover Hernani, a Spanish brigand and disinherited nobleman. Few spectators could miss the association of the desolate old man and the aging French monarch, Charles X.

A group of offended Classicist playwrights immediately petitioned the king, asking him to ban all Romantic plays at the Comédie Française. When that effort failed, members of the Académie Française mobilized against the play. Meanwhile, brigades of youthful Romanticists rose in Hugo's defense. His supporters mobilized to find their way into the theater to lend their vocal (and at times physical) support. The battle lines swirling around *Hernani* had been joined.

At just about 1:00 pm on the afternoon of the opening performance—February 25, 1830—lines formed surrounding the theater, closing nearby streets. Sporting long hair, beards, vintage clothing, padded jackets, and purplish velvet, the assembling swarm appeared unlike the usual well-groomed Comédie Française audience members of old. Those who could forced their way in before the police sealed off the theater at 3:00 pm.

With hours before the 7:00 pm curtain time, the intruders settled in for a long wait, chowing down on whatever food they had managed to sneak in concealed in their clothing. When offended usherettes refused to unlock the bathrooms, audience members relieved themselves on the auditorium floor. Theater staff went to the roof and threw garbage onto the crowd below. Later arriving traditional ticket holders found filth and chaos as they tried to make their way to their seats.

Calm did not descend as the curtain rose. Throughout the performance, the various sides shouted, booed, sang, and punched one another. The young Romantics won the hour, as the Classicists in the audience beat a hasty retreat home. The battles continued throughout the play's thirty-nine-performance run, with audience members storming the stage, and the actors on many nights performing behind a line of soldiers, while some in the hall were bayoneted in the process. Conservative commentators railed against lunatics and devil-worshippers in the audience; their liberal counterparts vilified intransigent guardians of an old order.

Hugo would go on to become one of France's most illustrious authors; the Comédie Française remained among France's most hallowed theater companies. Charles X did not fare so well. Within weeks of the curtain coming down on *Hernani*'s final performance, he was run out of the country in what became known as the July Revolution. Charles would die in Austrian exile a half-dozen years later. The new king, Louis-Philippe I, who would reign until the next revolution eighteen years later, marked the ascendency of a rising bourgeoise and new monied classes, which, in their own ways, represented the anthesis of both Old Royalist Classicists and Revolutionary Romanticists.

Fundamentally, the turmoil swirling around the premier of Hugo's *Hernani* reflected the arrival of a new aesthetic, together with its creators. The arts were changing, as were their audiences. France was changing, as was Paris. The old and new fell into disputation, which ended up by obliterating the Old Regime and its remaining supporters. A new France, Paris, and theater emerged in its place.

New Cities, New Arts

As this tale of early-nineteenth-century Paris and its theater culture illustrates, cities constantly change, as do the performing arts. Form, tastes, structural supports, economic realities, and political regimes all influence how cities, and the arts, evolve. So, too, do cities and the arts shape one another, especially at moments when change is happening at an accelerating pace. This volume explores the dynamic relationship between urban and artistic transformation; and it does so both by visiting the emergence of new performing arts institutions at moments when both urban growth and artistic evolution appear to be accelerating; and by discussing those moments when changes on stage promote a broader transformation of their cities and communities.

More specifically, this volume examines these relationships through a limited number of case studies revealing in more detail how such change occurs both in cities and in theaters. The next four chapters chart the emergence of Montreal as a major center of performance dance, in tandem with Quebec's secularizing "Quiet Revolution"; the transformation of Washington's theater scene that accompanied the city's makeover from congressional fiefdom to home-ruled metropolitan hub; the rise of Toronto's stridently self-reverential theater community in accord with its growth from a provincial backwater of empire to national preeminence; and efforts in Kyiv after independence to reclaim a theater history that had been obliterated by authoritarian rule.

The influence of a changing city on its artistic scene can be direct. How cities define and consolidate themselves shapes audiences, funding sources, and legal institutions that determine how arts organizations exist and mature. The initial essays chart how these local externalities determine the ways in which residents pursuing the arts can do so. The effect of new performing styles and institutions on their cities is more diffuse, perhaps ethereal. By pursuing artistic expression and the organizational structures supporting it, theatrical entrepreneurs give symbolic and institutional form to what it means to be part of their cities. By examining moments of observable variation, these essays bear witness to the powerful relationship between cities and their artistic institutions.

The final chapter examining Nashville reverses the causal arrows. Rather than examining instances when urban change fostered new creativity in the performing arts, the final case study exposes how the performing arts can transform their cities. Indeed, the arts attract attention, residents, and investment beyond whatever a city might otherwise have drawn.

All too often, we regard the performing arts either as a pleasant add-on to more serious aspects of life or as an economic engine generating income and driving economic development. The arts, of course, can be both; but their connection to our primal selves adds an additional—often-underappreciated—dimension.

Dancing to a New Identity

Chapter 2 explores the transformation of Montreal. Turning to the connection between urban change and the emergence of new artistic institutions, Quebec came out of World War II stuck in a time warp that placed La Belle Province at odds with much of North America. For more than a century, the province languished under a brokered allocation of colonial power that stymied its entrance into the contemporary world.[2] An Anglophone Protestant elite controlled the commanding heights of commerce from their imposing stone citadels. Spread out in fifty shades of gray granite, their control centers stretched along the downtown littoral of Mount Royal from McGill University to Windsor Station, where the commuter trains sat ready to whisk them away at 5:00 pm.[3]

French-speaking, black-robed Catholic clergy controlled the rest of the province, keeping their flock tied to the countryside for farming or, in many instances, the messier task of resource extraction. A nationalistic right-wing populist government under Premier Maurice Duplessis and his thuggish Union Nationale Party—together with corrupt police and officialdom—used its gerrymandered majority in the Assemblée Nationale to ensure that little would change.[4]

Transformation came as the rest of the continent increasingly developed into what would grow in a few years into the most dynamically mobile continental economy in world history. Even the forces of traditionalism so prevalent in Quebec could not resist. After Duplessis's death, the old system snapped during the "Quiet Revolution" begun in 1960 by a new Liberal government under Jean Lesage. Modernity arrived in Quebec, unleashing intense sociopolitical and sociocultural adjustments accompanied by secularization, the creation of a welfare state, and incompatible federalist and sovereigntist factions. Identities and values radically loosened as Quebec went, according to numerous surveys, from being the most religious to the most secularized society in North America.[5]

Nothing escaped this transformation, including performance dance. Beginning almost immediately after World War II, those Montrealers connected to continental trends in the arts began to push back against the repressive policies of Duplessis and the Church.

New Montrealers debarking from war-torn Europe brought their cultural tastes and expectations with them. French-language television arrived in the 1950s, programmed by the federal government bent on destroying the priestly grip of Québécois traditionalists.

Before 1945, the only serious dance reaching Montreal stages was performed by visiting companies made up of Americans, Europeans, and displaced Russians (including Ruth St. Denis, Mary Wigman, Charles Weidman, Isadora Duncan, Anna Pavlova, and various legacy companies from Les Ballets Russes).[6] Dance, however, spoke to Montrealers across the city's deep linguistic divide between francophones and anglophones. By the 1960s, Montreal had its own classical company and the first of what would become a panoply of modern dance troupes.[7]

Claiming Presence Through Theater

Chapter 3 portrays the evolution of Washington, whose story begins when President George Washington named Thomas Jefferson as his first secretary of state. Several weeks after having been nominated for Washington's first Cabinet, Jefferson invited Treasury Secretary Alexander Hamilton and Virginia congressman James Madison to dinner at his New York City home. Beyond pleasantries, Jefferson sought to settle a noisome dispute over the location of the new country's capital city. The resulting Compromise of June 1790 followed, with southerners led by Madison agreeing to have the national government assume states' debt in exchange for the capital city decamping to the South.[8] The agreement took place in "The Room Where It Happened," which is featured prominently in Lin-Manuel Miranda's musical *Hamilton* two-and-a-quarter centuries later.[9]

President Washington and his commissioners set out the following spring to identify a site for the new city along the Potomac upriver from his plantation at Mount Vernon. The final agreement was reached with local landowners in a Georgetown tavern room (now preserved within Ukraine's Embassy to the United States) allotting a payment of $66.66 for each acre used by the capital. Major Pierre L'Enfant designed the 6,622-acre Federal

City on the basis of Louis XIV's design for Versailles.[10] Together with the African American surveyor Benjamin Banneker, L'Enfant planned sweeping avenues cut through forests, marshes, and plantations dependent on slave labor. Despite any number of problems—including L'Enfant's dismissal, offset by Banneker's steady professionalism—Congress moved to its new Capital in 1800, giving birth to Washington, DC.[11]

Aside from the tobacco ports of Alexandria and Georgetown, more of the "city" existed in L'Enfant's megalomaniacal mind than in reality. Retrocession to Virginia in 1846 of the lands south of the Potomac at the behest of Alexandria's slave merchants held out a model for abandoning the project altogether.[12] The city, however, grew as a front-line military encampment during the Civil War, and its status as capital was cemented by the martyrdom of President Abraham Lincoln at a local theater.

Congress retained control over the city, abolishing local home rule in 1874. For the next ninety-nine years, the city operated under the control of congressionally appointed commissioners dominated by officers of the Army Corps of Engineers.[13] The city remained primarily a governmental and administrative center throughout these decades. This status began to change as the United States emerged from World War II.

The US government rapidly expanded during the 1940s and 1950s, as the "Welfare State" grew domestically and the "Security State" expanded internationally in response to the Cold War. As elsewhere in America, city residents began an exodus to the suburbs, a movement accelerated by the end of legal racial segregation in housing. By the late 1950s, Washington became the first major US city with an African American majority. The city was surrounded by predominantly white, middle-class suburbs increasingly defined by interstate highways, such as its surrounding Beltway.[14]

Further changes were afoot by the 1980s, as the city grew into a metropolitan region of some 6 million by the twenty-first century with an economy dominated by highly paid private-sector jobs in health and computer technology industries.[15] As local techies proudly proclaim, the internet was invented in the DMV ("District-Maryland-Virginia") and not in California.

These profound transformations included the growth of a significant community of highly educated professionals who sought out the arts. These professionals – be they government workers, lawyers and lobbyists, medical or high tech researchers – provided a cultivated base with plentiful funds for the arts absent in most other American cities. Once a theatrical wasteland, Washington began to nurture inventive theater companies, with the region growing by 2020 into the second-largest theater market in the country.[16]

The Washington Theater Club was a pioneer among these newcomers, operating between 1957 and 1974.[17] Over the course of a decade and a half, the club staged ninety Equity (union) productions and ten non-Equity shows, including ten world premieres, four American premieres, and thirty Washington premieres. During the mid-1960s, the company produced up to one quarter of all new works staged in American regional theaters. The club served as a proving ground for actors starting their careers, including several who would come to dominate the American stage and screen. Founded as an artistic expression of social activism, the club promoted Black theater and Black writers and artists. Despite artistic success, the club succumbed to financial constraints, internal conflicts, and the hostility of a local pre–home rule regime accountable to Congress rather than city residents. The club's story became intwined with changes that were transpiring throughout a city fighting to liberate itself from congressional control through home rule.

Unleashing Diversity from the Stage

Chapter 4 describes the postwar transformation of Toronto. At the end of World War II, Toronto retained its reputation as "America's Belfast." Beset almost from its founding by sectarian conflict and violence among predominantly "Orange" English, Scotch, and Irish Protestant community members embedded in Britain's colonial system and a largely "Republican" Irish Catholic immigrant working class, the city had a nasty reputation. The thuggish mentality of the Protestant Orange Lodges dominated the city's story throughout its first century and a half, which began in 1793 when Governor John Graves Simcoe relocated Upper Canada's colonial capital for protection against American aggression. As late as 1955, the city's mayor, Leslie Howard Saunders, promoted Toronto as a Protestant bastion. There was nothing subtle about his message. Saunders listed himself in his campaign materials as "Protestant."[18]

Unsurprisingly, Toronto's soot-covered brick cityscape often seemed to glower under low, gray Canadian skies. A deeply provincial industrial colonial outpost, Toronto seemingly lacked the dynamism of its as-yet-flourishing rust belt partners across the border to the south (e.g., Rochester, Buffalo, Cleveland, Toledo, and Detroit). As industry grew, the local real estate market relegated thousands of working-class families—often Irish Catholics supporting the Hibernian Benevolent Society in opposition to the Orange Lodges—to substandard homes in neighborhoods such as "Cabbagetown." Their highly idiosyncratic, self-built homes lent a higgly-piggly feel to many a proletarian street.[19]

Perhaps most irritating for the local creative class, local ordinances shut down all manner of sporting and cultural events on Sundays, while limiting the consumption of alcohol in public. There would be no traditional stand-up bars in "Toronto the Good" until the 1960s because alcohol consumption was prohibited without the purchase of food.[20] Those Torontonians who wished to drink at home had to apply for a government-issued license to purchase alcohol. The Polish physicist Leopold Infeld, who collaborated with Albert Einstein and Max Born during his career, perhaps best captured the city's atmosphere. Reflecting on his time teaching at the University of Toronto during the 1940s, Infeld observed that "it must be good to die in Toronto. The transition between life and death would be continuous, painless, and scarcely noticeable."[21]

A robust, largely Eastern European Jewish immigrant community proved to be the first harbinger of change when it arrived during the early years of the twentieth century. Largely concentrated at the foot of Spadina Avenue in an area dominated by the needle trades and nearby Kensington Market, Toronto's first Jewish residents were impoverished, having traveled more or less directly from the harsh *shtetls* of the Russian Empire.[22] Both Orange and Catholic Torontonians greeted them unkindly, a hostility exemplified by the infamous August 1933 Christie Pits Riots, which erupted when National Socialist wannabe Swastika Clubs attacked "foreigners" at a baseball game between Jewish and Italian community teams.[23]

World War II transformed the city forever. The war solidified the presence of the city's financial institutions, which were increasingly huddled around a portion of Bay Street dubbed by dispossessed Western farmers just a few years before as "Canada's Wall Street." The city's industrial base expanded, as Toronto became one of the chief shop floors for the British war effort. The war similarly nurtured the nascent communications sector, which would grow to rival similar hubs across North America. A young city in a young country, Toronto was ready for change.[24]

Immigrants were beginning to make their presence felt in new ways. More successful members of the Jewish community began to move uptown—and uphill—to the small, independent, wealthy enclave of Forest Hills. The floodgates of Italian immigration were about to open, luring tens of thousands of those impoverished by war. Moreover, English Canada began to integrate into a booming continental postwar American economy untouched by the ravages of war.

Still tied politically, economically, and psychologically to the imperial Mother Ship in London, Toronto nonetheless was beginning to create its own identity. The domination of Protestant hardliners organized around the Orange Lodges continued to exert control over public institutions; as did the imperial "Old Compact" families that had forged the Canadian confederation less than a century earlier and were now housed in neighborhoods with names such as "Rosedale."[25]

How is it, then, that a child born in postwar Toronto wakes up on any morning a lifetime later as a resident of one of the most successfully diverse cities in the world? A city that has become one of the English-speaking world's most vibrant theater towns, no less.[26] Chapter 4 examines these changes through the creation of Toronto's astonishing alternative theater scene during the 1960s and 1970s.

From Provincial City to International Capital

Chapter 5 explores Kyiv's growth from provincial city to international capital. Ancient Kyiv, founded over a millennium and a half ago, simultaneously is a young city. The city's glory days were long past, when the city passed to Russian suzerainty after the 1654 Treaty of Pereyaslav. The Russian Orthodox Church attained considerable daily control of the city to protect of some of Orthodox Christianity's holiest pilgrimage sites. Russian expansion to the south begun under Catherine II elevated the city's importance to imperial powers in Saint Petersburg. The city emerged as an important religious, educational, and military center throughout the nineteenth century, as its role as a logistical hub of empire grew ever more important.[27]

Kyiv thrived as a transportation and industrial center by the end of the nineteenth century, growing to about 130,000 residents, the vast majority of whom spoke Russian. Beyond ethnic Russians, the local population included significant Ukrainian, Jewish, and Polish communities. The city suffered greatly with the collapse of imperial authority in 1917. Over the next five years, the city changed hands among Red and White Russian forces, Ukrainian nationalist legions, and German and Polish armies eighteen times. Recovery proved anemic until the Soviet government moved the capital of the Ukrainian Soviet Socialist Republic from Kharkiv in 1934. Kyiv leveraged its new status to emerge as a significant industrial center by the time the Wehrmacht crossed the Soviet-Polish border in June 1941.[28]

The city found itself on the front lines, having been occupied by the German invaders, who were later driven out by the Red Army. The German occupiers exterminated the city's Jewish population—including murdering over 33,000 Jews at the Babyn Yar ravine between September 29 and 30, 1941. In all, the German army is thought to have massacred between 100,000 and 150,000 Jews, prisons of war, communists, and Romani people at Babyn Yar between September 1941 and the city's liberation by the Soviet Army in November 1943.[29]

The Soviet government rebuilt Kyiv as a showcase after the war. The city's status as a republic capital heightened its cultural and economic importance. Ukraine even became one of the founding members of the United Nations, making Kyiv theoretically an international capital. The city became the Soviet Union's third-largest and one of its most productive, with an economy revolving around defense industries, scientific research, and administration. The city's population grew to over 2.5 million by the end of the Soviet period. While Ukrainians now constituted the largest ethnic group, the city remained primarily Russian speaking.[30]

Politically and culturally, late Soviet Kyiv was a city more partitioned than it appeared. Concerned with rising Ukrainian nationalism, late Soviet leaders in Moscow discouraged use of the Ukrainian language and exercised control over the smallest hints of nationalistic intent. Discontent—economic, philosophical, and linguistic—percolated out of view. The April 1986 nuclear accident at the Chernobyl Nuclear Power Plant 60 miles north of Kyiv became an inflection point. Growing concern accompanied rumors of the disaster, especially after local Communist Party leaders went ahead with the planned May Day demonstrations and parades a few days later. Kyiv's population was no longer quiescent and loyal. Increasingly, city residents wanted as little to do as possible with the Soviet Union.[31]

On a warm July 1990 day, as a crowd of perhaps 30,000 or 40,000 watched, a lone Kyiv city council deputy purposefully walked through City Hall's front door, having heard that the republic's Verkhovna Rada had adopted a declaration on state sovereignty a few minutes before. Climbing lampposts, clambering atop city buses, running every which way—thousands upon thousands watched in anticipation and disbelief as the young man approached the city's official flagpole. Slowly, the Soviet hammer-and-sickle came down, followed by a few fumbling movements. A spray of blue-and-yellow began to flow from the deputy's hands. With every hoist higher, the rising banner of an as-yet-not-fully born independent Ukraine unfolded into view. As the blue-and-yellow flag rose skyward, many in the crowd understood that they were no longer Soviet.[32] By December 1991, Kyiv would be the capital of an independent Ukraine. Theater artists now were free to tell their own stories as they wished.

Music Makes the Town

Chapter 6 explores burgeoning Nashville. As recently as 1960, very little distinguished Nashville from any number of medium-sized American cities. Nashville hardly stood out among American state capitals, themselves a rather undistinguished grouping of urban communities. For much of its history, the city rested comfortably according to various measures of urbanity among other state capitals, such as Columbus (Ohio), Montgomery (Alabama), Raleigh (North Carolina), Sacramento (California), and Trenton (New Jersey). Only a few capitals—such as Atlanta (Georgia), Boston (Massachusetts), Saint Paul and neighboring Minneapolis (Minnesota), and perhaps Pheonix (Arizona), Denver (Colorado), and Indianapolis (Indiana)—differentiated themselves at the time as worthy of a second look as a metropolitan center of any significance.

Not much about Nashville seemed noteworthy, aside from William Crawford Smith's full-scale replica of the original Parthenon in Athens built in 1897, a more distinguished local university scene than most (including two denominational schools founded in the aftermath of the Civil War, for whites—Vanderbilt University—and Blacks—Fisk University), a particularly powerful radio station, and a long and continuing history of white supremacist ideology and African American resistance. That radio station, however, turns out to have changed the city's trajectory entirely. The city's population remained stagnant, even falling during the 1960s, before its unprecedented growth throughout the 1970s that catapulted the city and region into an entirely different urban category.[33]

James Robertson and John Donelson founded the city in 1779 at the site of an earlier settlement of French fur traders and Native American campgrounds. Established during the American Revolution as one of the first settlements west of the Appalachian Mountains, its founders named their modest community for the Continental Army's General Francis Nash.[34] These early settlers would capitalize over time on the site's convenient location for river transportation. This ease of transportation led to the city being named the permanent capital of Tennessee in 1843. The coming of the railroads during the mid–nineteenth century solidified this advantage, encouraging the formation of a small but robust manufacturing center and various subsidiary financial institutions after the Civil War.

By the first quarter of the twenty-first century, Nashville anchored a metropolitan region of more than 2 million inhabitants that had become an economic powerhouse, emerging as one of the fastest-growing metropolitan regions in the country, home to offices of dozens of *Fortune* 500 companies, one of the country's largest concentrations of health care companies, and several major automobile plants.[35] The city's music industry stands at the center of this explosive growth.

By the 1920s, Edwin Craig, the son of the founder of the National Life and Accident Insurance Company, took note of the success of rising radio stations around the country that were attracting listeners by featuring an amalgamation of roots music that record companies were branding "Hillbilly Music." Businessmen launched radio stations in Kansas City (KFKB), Iowa (KFNF), and Chicago (WLS) at the dawn of the new broadcast industry (Pittsburgh's KDKA having secured the nation's first broadcast license in 1920). Craig convinced his skeptical father to set up a studio, which began broadcasting under the call letters WSM (for "We Shield Millions") in October 1925.[36]

To the horror of his family and social equals, Craig recruited George D. Hay from Chicago's WLS to take over programming. Hay garnered the title of America's favorite announcer broadcasting on the Windy City's powerful new station, where he brought the sounds and music of everyday America to listeners. Hay planned to end WSM's rather staid programming, ranging from Vivaldi to popular tunes. Within a month of the station's inaugural broadcast, Hay was scheduling white fiddler "Uncle Jimmy" Thompson and Black harmonica player DeFord Bailey, establishing a new program format: *WSM Barn Dance*. The show soon would be renamed *The Grand Ole Opry*.

This new format led Craig and Hay to build connections throughout the region's music community, drawing in undiscovered performers as well as those recently recorded by the Victor Talking Machine Company and the breakaway OKeh label. The station sent these musical groups on tours into the surrounding hinterlands to attract attention and, more importantly, sell insurance policies. Nevertheless, the Nashville station was not sufficiently powerful to compete with Atlanta's powerhouse WSB and the ever-more-powerful WLS, broadcasting from Chicago.

WSM's—and Nashville's—trajectory changed during the early 1930s. Radio audiences expanded as the new media attracted thousands of listeners to its free format as Depression-era privations began to bite into disposable income. Craig and the National Life and Accident Insurance Company successfully bid on one of only three federal licenses in the South for powerful 50,000 watt "clear channel" broadcasting.[37]

The Grand Ole Opry show emerged as WSM's signature broadcast, winning fans throughout the South and beyond (listeners could tune in across thirty states, primarily on the East Coast). With the station's studios no longer able to accommodate the expanding audience, it moved to ever-larger venues, such as the Hillsboro Theatre, the Dixie Tabernacle, and the War Memorial Auditorium.

In June 1943, WSM set up shop in the Ryman Auditorium (the former Union Gospel Tabernacle), which had begun hosting nonreligious shows, lectures, and sporting events during the early twentieth century to pay off debts. *The Opry* remained at the Ryman until 1974, when the country show moved to the special-built Opryland entertainment complex east of town.[38]

The show, radio station, and auditorium became hubs around which the new country music industry grew. By the twenty-first century, Nashville had become a leader within the music and recording worlds, regularly ranked first, second, or third with New York and Los Angeles, depending on the indices. Music made Tennessee's modest capital into a major global cultural center. If previous stories reveal how growing cities spawn new theater and dance scenes, music made the town in Nashville.

The first four case studies that follow illustrate how urban growth creates new wealth and nurtures the audiences necessary to support the arts. In each instance, the arts, in turn, help communities work through the divisions of language, race, generational change, and postcolonialism. The fifth case demonstrates how the success of the performing arts—especially of a commercialized performing art form, such as country music—can elevate a city to previously unimagined heights.

Chapter 2

Montreal: Moving Center Stage — Dance and Modernization in the Late Twentieth Century

Quebec came out of World War II stuck in a time warp that placed La Belle Province at odds with much of North America. Transformation came as the rest of the continent increasingly became incorporated into what would grow in a few years into the most dynamically mobile continental economy in world history.[39] Even the forces of traditionalism so prevalent in Quebec could not resist. Nothing escaped this transformation, including performance dance.

The opening bell in the culture wars against clerical hegemony came in August 1948, when the artistic manifesto titled *Le Refus Global*, issued by a handful of artists, propelled a new vision for Quebec culture.[40] This proclamation was the brash cry of abstract artists influenced by the French surrealists. Enraged at the "cassocks that have remained the sole repositories of faith, knowledge, truth, and national wealth," the group took on the title Les Automatistes.

In August 1948, sixteen of their number composed and self-published a manifesto proclaiming the "untamed need for liberation," "resplendent anarchy," and extolling the creative force of the subconscious. Mimeographed in four hundred copies, their platform, *Le Refus Global*, sold for a dollar a copy at a local Montreal bookstore. This seemingly obscure artistic declaration set the tone for intense cultural debates to follow. The twenty-three-year-old dancer, choreographer, painter, and sculptor Françoise Sullivan was among the sixteen signatories.[41]

Sullivan had grown up in Montreal, trained in classical dance by Gérald Crevier. She studied painting at École des beaux-arts de

Montréal, where she became friends with the abstract painter Paul-Émile Borduas and others among Les Automatistes.⁴² In 1945 she moved to New York, where she delved into modern dance with Franziska Boas, Martha Graham, and Louis Horst. Returning to her native city in 1948, Sullivan performed with Jean-Paul Riopelle and Maurice Perron in a snow-covered field near Mont-St. Hilaire in what proved to be a landmark work in Quebec modern dance: *Danse dans la neige* (*Dance in the Snow*).⁴³

As Sullivan's career reveals, Les Automatistes emerged just as the modern age burst forth in Quebec. Economic and political transformation swept away the old order dominated by Anglo-economic and Franco-clerical power; new technologies and the arrival of postwar immigrants transformed the possibilities for cultural renewal. Dance would become a major arena for this change; and television would bring it to the forefront of cultural transformation.

Television broadcasting in Canada is an expensive undertaking, given the country's vast distances punctuated by relatively few settlements and cities of size. Initial telecasts began in Montreal and Toronto in September 1952, with the first national service following in 1958.⁴⁴ This expansive public enterprise paralleled similar public radio broadcasting systems that emerged in the 1930s as a nation-wide accompaniment to localized commercial stations. These government efforts provided important shared content to all Canadians. Public media also offered a counterweight to the powerful American radio and television networks leaking across the border.

The challenges confronting English-language broadcasting in Canada were magnified in the French service. Audiences were smaller and more dispersed; and readily available content proved more difficult to find. The task of creating a distinctively French-language Québécois television fell to Radio-Canada in Montreal.⁴⁵

Working within a limited budget, producers turned to the local performing arts community for content. Montreal playwrights and actors created madly popular drama and comedy series, such as *La famille Plouffe*, based on a novel by Roger Lemelin.⁴⁶ Set in a working-class Quebec family, this and other shows brought Quebec's daily life and language to the screen. These efforts provided steady employment for Montreal's writers, directors, actors, and musicians—an important safety net that enabled survival in an otherwise harsh economic environment.⁴⁷

Beyond drama, variety shows came to be a convenient way to fill time by promoting local comedians, musicians, and dancers. Given the uncongenial climate for dance, producers found they had to rely on many dance professionals who had immigrated from abroad or who had disguised their Québécois identity behind made-up foreign—usually Russian-sounding—names.

The Founders

Maurice Lacasse, the son of a ballroom dance teacher and grandson of a legendary folk violinist, was born in Montreal in 1906. His father, Adelard, moved to the city and became a schoolteacher after having been forced to leave the family's country home a few years before Maurice was born. Adelard's patrons raised money to send him to New York to learn the latest crazes—such as the Waltz and Cakewalk—where he studied with Irene and Vernon Castle before returning to make his living at a Saint Lawrence Boulevard dance studio. Maurice grew up surrounded by dance and music.[48]

At twenty, Maurice ran off with a Frenchwoman—Carmen Sierra—who was a year his senior. After eloping, Maurice and Carmen connected with a company of Russian balalaika musicians and dancers. The group invited Maurice and Carmen to join them when one of their acts fell to injury. Their combination of toe, tap, and acrobatic dancing became an instant hit, and the couple embarked on a five-year North American tour. It was during this time that Maurice—like many North American–born dancers—changed his name to the Russian-sounding Morenoff to try to associate with the success of Diaghilev's Ballets Russes.[49]

The Morenoffs returned to Montreal in 1931 as the Great Depression set in. They opened a dance studio and library in a triplex in Montreal's east end that would remain a fixture on the Montreal dance scene until their deaths in the early 1990s (Carmen in 1990; and Maurice in 1993). The couple trained the first generation of French Canadian male dancers, including Fernand Nault, Roland Lorrain, Marc Beaudet, and Michel Boudot.[50]

Their contemporary, Gérard Crevier, was born in Longueuil, Quebec, in 1912 to a French Canadian father and Irish mother.

Crevier fell in love with dance at the age of ten after seeing Anna Pavlova dance at the Orpheum Theatre. Pavlova inspired the young boy to enroll in Ezzak Ruvenoff's dance school, where he studied ballet while being instructed in tap by Dora Marshall, who would dance at Radio City Music Hall in New York. His dance career began by filling in the intermissions between shows at local movie theaters. He would marry Elisabeth "Zette" Devaux, a dancer from the French West Indies, and head off to England at the age of twenty to join the corps de ballet of the Sadler's Wells Company.[51]

Crevier started teaching in Montreal during the 1930s before returning to Europe in the Canadian Army during World War II. Andrée Millaire, Lise Gagnier, and Françoise Sullivan were among his students. He organized successful recitals and, after the war, brought the Royal Academy of Dance ballet syllabus back to the city. His small company, featuring his own choreography, appeared widely after the war, including the highly successful performance at the third Canadian Ballet Festival held in Montreal in 1950.[52] Crevier's Les Ballets-Québec folded in 1952, after which he briefly joined the new National Ballet of Canada in Toronto before relocating to Venice, Florida, and leaving the dance world.[53]

Montreal dance's third seminal figure, Ludmilla (Otzup-Gorny) Chiriaeff, came to Montreal as an immigrant from war-torn Europe in 1952. Chiriaeff was born to Russian parents in Riga in 1924 and grew up in Berlin, studying with former dancers from the Bolshoi. Michel Fokine was among the many prominent émigré Russian artists and performers who passed through the exiled family's home in the German capital. Chiriaeff performed small roles in Colonel de Basil's *Ballets Russes* and continued dancing throughout World War II, ending up in Geneva. Marrying Russian set designer Alexis Chiriaeff, she taught ballet, danced with local companies on stage, and appeared in the film *Danse Solitaire*.[54]

Chiriaeff arrived in Montreal in the middle of the frigid 1951–52 winter. Stepping out for a breath of air on her first evening in town, she saw her name in the lights. *Danse Solitaire* happened to be showing in a theater down the street from her hotel. Her love affair with Montreal was sealed.[55] She began teaching dance and formed her own group—Les Ballets Chiriaeff—in response to the insatiable demand for content by Montreal television. These shows introduced local audiences to performance dance.

Chiriaeff already had secured an enthusiastic audience for her group before ever stepping onto a theater stage as Les Grands Ballets Canadiens in 1957. Now named more grandly, the company performed to solid reviews at the Jacob's Pillow summer season in Massachusetts and elsewhere across Canada. She recruited French Canadian dancers—including Fernand Nault, who had been working with the American Ballet Theatre in New York—and reached out to the Roman Catholic Church, performing religiously inspired programs in prominent Montreal churches.[56]

These activities established a strong connection between her company and the emerging French-Canadian identity. This association deepened in the future, as she expanded her efforts to include a school and a library, which provided an all-important institutional base for the Montreal dance community. By the 1960s, Les Grands Ballets Canadiens had joined with the Royal Winnipeg Ballet and the National Ballet of Canada as the country's triumvirate of classical dance.[57]

The Morenoffs, Crevier, and Chiriaeff teamed up with other immigrants who brought international dance culture to French Canada during the middle years of the twentieth century. These included Ruth Sorel, who was born to Polish parents—the Abramowitz family—in Germany in 1907; Elizabeth Leese; and Séda Zaré.

Sorel had launched a well-regarded career in Germany—including a turn with the Berlin Opera under Bruno Walter—before the Nazis came to power in 1933. She left for Poland, established her own school, and toured internationally before marrying the playwright Michel Choromanski. Sorel eventually made her way to Montreal in 1944, where she opened a dance studio at the Westmont YMCA and formed a small modern group in the German expressionist tradition. She choreographed new ballets drawing on Quebec and Canadian themes—such as *La Gaspesienne* (1949)—and took her dancers to New York as well as across Canada. The couple returned to Poland in the mid-1950s.[58]

Elizabeth Leese, the child of an academic family of mixed Danish and German heritage, was born in 1916. She studied modern dance in Germany before receiving classical training in Paris with former Saint Petersburg teachers. Joining the Swiss Trudi Schoop modern dance company, Leese traveled to North America for the first time in 1937. Eventually ending up in England, she married a Canadian journalist, Kenneth Johnstone, and settled in Toronto in 1939. Entering a Toronto dance scene dominated by the Russian émigré Boris Volkoff, she carved out a distinctive place for herself promoting modern dance.

In 1944, Leese and Johnstone moved to Montreal and began spending time in New York, where she took courses from Martha Graham, Doris Humphrey, and Hanya Holm, Antony Tudor, Margaret Craske, Edward Caton, and George Balanchine. Moving easily among Montreal's language communities, she operated a successful school. She taught at both McGill and the Université de Montréal, and she formed the Montreal Theatre Ballet with her student Brian MacDonald. By 1960, she had become associated with Les Grands Ballets, where she remained until she died too young from cancer in 1962.[59]

Séda Zaré was born in 1911 to a successful Armenian family involved in the Baku oil trade. Her family fled to England in 1921 after the Turkish massacre of Armenians and the Bolshevik Revolution. There, she went to boarding school, studied ballet with Nicolas Legat, and free dance with Margaret Morris and J. Gordon Denning. She eventually left for Paris to become a student of Boris Kniaseff, before moving to Germany. A favored student of Alexandra Nikolaeva in Berlin, Zaré took over Nikolaeva's school upon her teacher's retirement. A young Ludmilla Chiriaeff began studying dance at the school during these years.

Changing her name during the war in response to Nazi suspicion, Zaré enjoyed a successful dance career and toured widely throughout Europe once the war ended. She and her family emigrated to Canada as war refugees in 1950. She opened Russian-style schools in Montreal, Trois Rivieres, and Shawinigan, producing students such as Bernadette Beliveau and Marie Cote, who would enjoy successful professional careers in Toronto, Lille, and elsewhere. She also launched a successful collaboration with the City of Montreal's Parks and Recreation Service, which brought creative dance to a broader public.[60]

The Montreal dance pioneers Sullivan, Crevier, the Morenoffs, Sorel, Leese, and Zaré provided a durable foundation for the city's vibrant and abundant dance scene. They extended roots from the rather barren Quebec cultural landscape—which for far too long had been dominated by clerical traditionalists who excoriated dance as immoral—deeply into some of the most bountiful among the century's dance scenes, including Berlin, Paris, London, New York, and, by extension, Moscow, Saint Petersburg, and Kyiv. Drawing fresh energy from the social and political upheavals that were sweeping across the city and province at the dawn of the 1960s, these pioneers created a fresh and distinctive Montreal dance culture that they could call their own.

Les Grands Ballet Canadiens

The move of Les Ballets Chiriaeff from the television studio to the theatrical stage and its accompanying metamorphosis into Les Grands Ballets Canadiens marks a moment of consolidation for Montreal dance. Montreal performance dance now claimed a core institution that would grow into a complete unit, with a high-quality school and research facility. Les Grands Ballets provided a touchstone for homegrown talent, as well as a point of connection with the larger dance world, through which accomplished artists were drawn to the city and Montreal dance journeyed out into the world.

By joining the ranks of Canada's top classical companies together with the Royal Winnipeg Ballet and the National Ballet of Canada, Les Grands Ballets arrived at just the right moment to become an institution of Canadian significance.[61] Emerging as it did as a French-language-oriented institution as Quebec nationalism took flight, the company cemented a powerful place for itself in the French Canadian imagination. Les Grands Ballets provided the bedrock on which the diverse and dynamic performance dance scene could grow.

In 1962, the Canada Council—the federal government's grant-making agency for the arts—attempted to untangle the adversarial relationships that had grown up among the three dominant classical companies.[62] The council's arts supervisor, Peter Dwyer, commissioned a survey and evaluation of the Canadian dance scene by Lincoln Kirstein, cofounder of the New York City Ballet, and the British ballet critic Richard Buckle. Noting the Russian traditions of Les Grands Ballets, Kirstein recommended that Canadian ballet start over again with Montreal as a focal point. Council bureaucrats ignored this recommendation and continued funding all three companies—due, no doubt, to administrative and political exigencies. [63]

Chiriaeff built her company from an original troupe of sixteen dancers by melding her school with the company. In 1958, she reorganized her dance studio into the Académie des Grands Ballets Canadiens to prepare performers for her company. In 1970, that institution grew into L'École supérieure de danse du Québec, a foundational training center which—together with important programs at l'Univèrsité du Québec à Montréal (l'UQÀM), Concordia University, and l'Université de Montréal—form the core for dance education in the city and province. Chiriaeff stepped down as Les Grands Ballets artistic director in 1974 to devote her energies to the school.[64]

Chiriaeff assiduously drew on Montreal talent. She invited Fernand Nault to assume the artistic directorship of the company in 1965. Trained by Maurice Morenoff, Nault enjoyed success at the New York–based American Ballet Theatre beginning in 1944. In 1960, he retired from performing, assuming the directorship of the School of American Ballet. This experience proved crucial for advancing Chiariff's artistic and pedagogical aspirations for her company.

On stage, Nault choreographed an exciting version of *Slaughter on Tenth Avenue* for CBC Television, which featured him dancing together with Elizabeth Leese. His *Carmina Burana*, performed at the Expo '67 World's Fair—and his choreography for The Who's rock opera *Tommy*—brought the company a wildly enthusiastic younger following both at home and abroad. These successes enhanced box office revenues as well as winning a worldwide fan base, thereby placing Les Grands Ballets on the international map.[65]

No Less a Revolution for Being Quiet

The social, political, and cultural forces unleashed by the "Quiet Revolution" secularized Quebec's identity and nationalism. The arts played a significant role in this transformation precisely because the process rested on the expression of public and private identities.[66] The theater community constituted a radicalizing vanguard pushing forward new voices who were striving to decipher the meaning of everyday experiences on stage.[67]

Chiriaeff's Les Grands Ballets Canadiens continued to grow throughout the period, solidifying both its organizational capacities and its artistic signature. In September 1963, the company became an anchor tenant for Mayor Jean Drapeau's ambitious performing arts center, Place des Arts, taking up permanent residence in the well-appointed Salle Wilfrid-Pelletier.[68] Simultaneously, Chiriaeff consolidated the company's internal organization and nurtured a dedicated and effective permanent administrative staff, whose members helped her expand every aspect of the company's operations.[69] Failing health forced her retirement in 1992, just a few years before her death in 1994 at the age of seventy-two.[70]

Chiriaeff was followed as artistic director between 1974 and 1978 by Brian MacDonald, who clarified and refined the company's image, leading successful international tours and producing legendarily popular works. Chiriaeff's previous investment in institutional development paid large dividends after MacDonald's departure, as, between 1978 and 1985, the company's artistic vision was successfully curated by committee for nine years before ballet mistress Linda Stearns assumed the helm in late 1987 as sole artistic director. An American, Lawrence Rhodes, followed in 1989, and he was succeeded by the Macedonian-born Gradimir Pankov a decade later, and by the Italian Ivan Cavallari in 2017.[71]

This constancy supported a commitment to original work, often commissioned from some of Canada's leading choreographers, who have garnered international renown for the company.[72] For example, MacDonald invited Fernand Nault on board as resident choreographer. During his time with the company, Nault took full advantage of dance joining theater, opera, and music as the main pillars of the World Festival program associated with Expo '67.

The company's ethos fit well with Quebec's uncertain political atmosphere and became part of a period of exceptional artistic volatility in Montreal and the province. Nonetheless, as Iro Valaskakis Tembeck tellingly concludes a 2004 essay exploring the complex dynamics of dance and Montreal politics that appeared in Selma Landen Odom and Mary Jane Warner's *Canadian Dance*, "Les Grands Ballets' broad artistic vision does not particularly reflect a Quebecois sensibility, either in choreographic treatment or in thematic concerns. Nevertheless, when the rise of nationalism spilled over onto the performing arts scene in Quebec, the company strategically required its dancers to alter their names to more French-sounding ones, because it had been unofficially denounced as not sufficiently representative of the French-Canadian identity. During the 1970s Sacha Belinsky became Alexandre Belin, Roslyn Faierstein was billed as Roseline Forrestter, and Sylvia Kinal became known as Sylvie Chevalier. If the previous generation headed by the Lacasse-Morenoffs had sought Russian sounding names to emulate Diaghilev, we now witness a fascinating reversal in this conscious gesture to Frenchify stage names."[73]

Tembeck goes on to note that Montreal's best-known 1980s dancers were in modern and experimental dance. The city's pulsating dance scene nonetheless rested on the solid base provided by Les Grands Ballets and its schools, which were joined by notable dance programs at several local universities. In the process, dance entered the city's cultural bloodstream, moving from precious stage art to public expression in the quickly changing society.

Formative Turns

Three contemporary dance companies took shape in the chaotic political, social, cultural, and artistic environment enveloping Montreal during the late 1960s and 1970s. Each helped fashion the foundation on which the city's innovative and vibrant dance community continues to swirl: Le Groupe de la Place Royale (1966; left Montreal from 1977 to 2009), Le Groupe Nouvelle Aire (1968–82), and Le Ballet Jazz de Montrèal (1972–present).

In 1966, Jeanne Renaud founded a new company named after a small Old Montreal square outside her studio. Le Groupe de la Place Royal quickly became a focal point for Canadian modern dance.[74]

Renaud had been a young admirer of Les Automatistes, and she had embraced the principals set forth in their 1948 manifesto

Le Refus Global, even though she was not herself a signatory to the historic petition.[75] Instead, she headed off to New York, Paris, and London to study with some of modern dance's formative creators, including Hanya Holm, Mary Anthony, and Merce Cunningham.

Renaud returned to her native Montreal in the late 1950s; and, by the mid-1960s, she was looking for ways to bring together her interests in modern dance movement, staging, decor, and costumes. Finding a dearth of opportunities, she founded her own company and school in 1966. To succeed, she had to take on a broad assortment of performance and administrative roles. Over the company's first half-dozen years, she created thirty-one works, which she performed in Montreal and across Canada and the United States.

Renaud did not limit her boundless energies to her own company. She also held a number of important arts administrative positions with the Canada Council, Quebec's Ministére des affairs culturelles, l'UQÀM, and Les Grands Ballets Canadiens, where she spent time as co-artistic director with Linda Stearns. She also found time to fit in teaching in New York as well as Paris and joined with Françoise Riopelle in establishing L'École de Danse Moderne de Montréal.

Renaud turned the artistic and leadership reins of Le Groupe over to Peter Boneham upon her departure from the company in 1971. Boneham attracted a number of talented younger dancers, including Jean-Pierre Perreault, who assumed greater responsibilities for running the company in the years ahead. Artistically, Le Groupe approached contemporary dance in ways pioneered at the time by Merce Cunningham; particularly by developing choreography independent of music. The resulting randomness enabled individual company members to demonstrate their personal artistic visions.

The company experimented with melding new technologies and movement, as in Perreault's *Les Dames aux Vaches* (1975), which was performed with projected images of cows (and, when on tour in Vancouver, in an actual cow pasture). Later, Boneham teamed with the soprano Pauline Vaillancourt to connect sung poetry to movement.[76] He continued these "opera for dancers" performances after the company moved to Ottawa in 1977.[77]

After becoming progressively frustrated with an inability to generate adequate funding in Montreal, Boneham relocated to

Ottawa, where the group established itself as a more open enterprise.[78] Renamed Le Group Dance Lab in 1988, the company and its attached training studios became a fixture on the Ottawa scene, gaining international renown and exerting considerable artistic influence over the Canadian national dance scene.[79] Securing more generous support from the Ontario provincial government than had been the case in Quebec, Boneham nurtured a generation of leading Canadian dancers and choreographers who constantly experimented with new forms, expanded their movement vocabulary, and explored the interaction between human movement and technology. However, the company could not survive Boneham's retirement in 2008, and ceased to exist the following year.[80]

The French immigrants Rose-Marie Lèbe and Martine Époque founded Le Groupe Nouvelle Aire in 1968 as an extracurricular activity for dance students enrolled in the l'Université de Montréal's physical education program.[81] While Le Groupe de la Place Royal was apolitical, Le Groupe Nouvelle Aire embraced and gave expression to the upheavals of the moment.[82] Époque charged the group with creating a "Québécois" dance vocabulary, which could be integrated into the program's curriculum. Lèbe and Époque recruited students from across the university, creating a safe place for the clash of diverse approaches to dance. Over time, those students more dedicated to dance came to dominate the company, encouraging innovative choreographers and reaching out to Québec composers. Paul-André Fortier, Édouard Lock, Ginette Laurin, Louise Lecavalier, Daniel Léveillé, and other future stalwarts of the Montreal dance community started their careers with Le Groupe.

Époque left to join the faculty at l'UQÀM in 1980, and the company ceased operations in 1982, formally dissolving five years later. She would go on to chair that university's dance program and would become a key figure in the Montreal dance community.[83] Her numerous contributions would include creating l'Agora de la danse.[84]

Fortier, who was a dancer in the company, formed his own group and, together with Daniel Jackson, established Montréal Danse. He emerged as a leading choreographer, working with several companies both at home and abroad, including Les Grands Ballets Canadiens. He also joined the l'UQÀM faculty. His ability to surround himself with top talent helped to attract some of the most impressive innovators in dance to the city.[85]

Laurin launched her career as a young dancer just as Le Groupe Nouvelle Aire began to perform. Having trained with such Montreal luminaries as Fernand Nault, Madame Voronova, and Marjorie Lambert, she studied improvisation in New York and worked at home as well as internationally. She would later produce major works with several Montreal companies, including Danse-Cité, Montréal Danse, and Les Grands Ballets Canadiens.

Daniel Léveillé became an important Montreal choreographer, working closely with new wave avant-garde dance makers and integrating sexuality into performances. Together with the company's other leading lights, Fortier, Laurin, and Léveillé became leaders driving contemporary dance in Montreal over several decades.

Édouard Lock took the company's exciting inventiveness abroad. Born in Casablanca, Lock enrolled at Concordia University, where he wanted to study film and literature. He matriculated just as the Concordia dance program was taking off. He studied with Nora Hemenway of Le Groupe de la Place Royale and others at Concordia, as well as with Merce Cunningham. By the late 1970s, he had begun to try choreography, often working with others on major projects, including works for Les Grands Ballets Canadiens.

Lock's career blossomed after he founded La La La Human Steps in 1980, where he would gain international recognition for choreographing the music of such rock musicians as David Bowie, Frank Zappa, and Skinny Puppy. The company has garnered praise around the world.[86]

Though short lived, Le Groupe Nouvelle Aire exerted a lasting influence over Montreal's dance culture. Its organizers, choreographers, and dancers became embedded in dance education, while the performers and choreographers extended the reach of contemporary dance in directions that demanded attention both at home and abroad. This success as a cultural incubator was rooted in a desire to participate in the larger cultural upheavals of the day by defining a new Québécois identity through movement. Like the battle over sovereignty, its impact outlasted the immediate struggles of the 1960s and 1970s.

A third essential group in the city—Le Ballets Jazz de Montréal—would become among the city's most successful cultural initiatives of the past half century. The company and its dance form—labeled "ballet jazz" by its primary creator, Eva von Gencsy—swept North America by storm and created a dance boom throughout Quebec. Schoolchildren, housewives, and professional dancers formed a vast network of dance schools and studios promoting a popular audience, which has continued to sustain the dance-crazed Québécois society long since notoriety has worn off. The company continues to be among Canada's most-traveled cultural enterprises, drawing avid audiences around the world.

Eva von Gencsy left her native Hungary for Canada in 1948. She previously enjoyed success, having been trained at V. G. Troyanoff's Russian Academy in Budapest before the outbreak of World War II. After the war, she joined the Salzburg Landes Theatre as a soloist. Then the Winnipeg Ballet lured her across the Atlantic. She soon earned accolades for her clean, perky, expressive, and endearing style.[87] After a fire destroyed the Winnipeg company's sets and costumes, Ludmilla Chiriaeff invited her to Montreal, where von Gencsy, like Chiriaeff, would find an enduring place in the North American dance world. A leading dancer in Les Ballets Chiriaeff, she gained an enthusiastic following from her television appearances. Von Gencsy left the company once it evolved into Les Grands Ballets Canadiens to continue working in television. By the late 1960s, she had become a beloved popular cultural figure and bestowed the title of best dancer by French Radio Canada.[88]

Von Gencsy devoted considerable energy to teaching. Already in 1953, she was an instructor at the Banff School of Fine Arts. A few years later, she discovered jazz as a dance form and began teaching what she came to call "jazz ballet" at Banff and, later, at the Saidye Bronfman Centre and Séda Zaré's Montreal Professional Dance Center. She used jazz as a means for adding spontaneity and joy to the dance studio. As the number of students and accolades grew, she decided to move the form to the stage. She joined the French immigrant Geneviève Salbaing and the Haitian immigrant Eddy Toussaint to establish a performing company, Le Ballets Jazz de Montréal.

While Toussaint would leave the company to form his own troupe a year later, von Gencsy and her partners successfully guided the company forward. Winning major notices in Paris, Varna, and elsewhere, von Gencsy regularly taught across Europe and North America.[89] She would be a towering figure in the Quebec dance community until her death in 2013 after a heart attack suffered at the age of eighty-nine while introducing two of her works at the company's fortieth-anniversary performance.[90]

Von Gencsy, Salbaing, and Toussaint—like von Gencsy and Chiriaeff—were immigrants open to fresh ideas at a time of unusual creativity and invention in Montreal. They shaped the city's dance community as a leading center for contemporary dance, and they engaged the complex artistic, political, and cultural currents washing over the city as the Quiet Revolution evolved into a political contest over Quebec's sovereignty.

These three successful contemporary dance companies of the 1960s and 1970s—Le Groupe de la Place Royale, Le Groupe Nouvelle Aire, and Les Ballets Jazz de Montréal—responded to the deep and profound identity conflicts of the era unleased by Quebec's modernization during its Quiet Revolution. Each represented a different face of those struggles. Le Groupe de la Place Royale remained dedicated to dance in its abstract form, eventually finding new fertile ground in Ontario. Le Groupe Nouvelle Aire became rooted in the sovereignty project of emerging secular nationalists. Les Ballets Jazz de Montréal drew on and, in turn, enriched an ever-less-traditional popular culture and society more intent on fun than piety.

Together, they insinuated dance into the center of a deep and profound battle for the hearts and minds of Montrealers. As the dance historian Tembeck observed in her exploration of politics and dance, Montreal's dance history "has proven that dance can very easily become the body politic."[91]

Divertissement Diversification

The 1980s and 1990s proved to be a period of diversification within the Montreal dance world, with artistic leaders and their companies striking off in multiple directions. Often, these efforts led to a global stage. As a result, one speaks of the Montreal dance scene as being among the most noteworthy in North America.

In 1980, the already-successful Édouard Lock, a member of Le Groupe Nouvelle Aire, formed a new company, Lock Danseurs, to perform his choreography, with his collaborator, the dancer Louise Lecavalier, as lead performer.[92] The company's production *Lily Marlène dans la jungle* opened to rave reviews in Montreal's Théâtre l'Eskabel before moving to the Kitchen in New York. The group evolved into La La La Human Steps, which remained one of Montreal's most successful contemporary dance companies until it closed in September 2015 due to financial difficulties.[93]

Lock and La La La Human Steps were products of a Montreal scene rooted in the evolution of the city's performance dance community, while simultaneously enjoying noteworthy success on the world stage. The company was formed just as the city's cultural community was reaching out, partially in response to Quebec's renewed search for identity after the political failure of the sovereignty movement. This was a moment of prodigious creative energy.[94] It also was a moment that demanded more talent—especially more dancers—to keep pace with the imaginations of its leaders, especially choreographers.

This insatiable demand prompted the dance-teacher-choreographer Linda Rabin and the dance teacher Candace Loubert to found l'École Linda Rabin Danse Moderne in downtown Montreal in 1981.[95] Montreal native Rabin was returning home after studying with José Limón, Betty Jones, and Anna Sokolow at Juilliard in New York. She had worked in Israel as well as choreographed works for Les Grands Ballets Canadiens and other companies around the world.[96] Loubert often drew on ritualistic dance traditions in India, Nepal, Japan, and Bali as she performed in Europe as well as with Les Grands Ballets Canadiens at home.[97]

Other companies followed, including Danse-Cité, a company founded by Daniel Soulières. He founded the company in 1983 to promote contemporary dance before turning it over to the choreographer Jean-Pierre Perreault. Soulières embraced dance after having completed his degree in psychology at l'Université de Montréal. Initially studying classical ballet, he turned to contemporary dance working with such leading teachers such as Peggy Baker, Peter Boneham, Linda Rabin, and Tassy Teekman. Soulières quickly became one of the most popular dancers in Montreal, performing an average of thirty-seven shows each year between 1977 and 1996. These productions included roles created for him by the choreographers James Kudelka, Françoise Sullivan, Jeanne Renaud, and Paul-André Fortier, among many. He himself choreographed and co-choreographed dozens of works.[98]

Around the same time, in 1986, Le Groupe Nouvelle Aire's Paul-André Fortier joined with Daniel Jackson to establish Montréal Danse to facilitate pioneering dance that challenges audiences and dancers together in an interactive relationship. Fortier choreographed works for Montréal Danse even as he continued to work with larger companies, including Les Grands Ballets Canadiens. He taught dance at l'UQÀM after his retirement from performances in 1989.[99]

Fortier and Jackson were innovative organizationally as well. Seeking to promote the company as a collective enterprise, they named no permanent choreographer.[100] Instead, the company deepened its commitment to partnerships with multiple cutting-edge artists. This perishability has lasted permanently for more than thirty years, with Montréal Danse retaining pride of place on the Montreal dance scene.

From *Le Refus Global* to La Danse Globale

The twenty-first century began with Montreal well established as a significant international center for performance dance, and a global leader in the two dance-related genres of physical theater and circus arts. One might have thought this always was so. However, just a half century before, Quebec's clerical arbiters of public taste had frowned on physical artistic expression in almost any form.

The emergence of first classical, then modern and contemporary, dance in Montreal is inexorably linked to broader changes in society that drove political conflict and deep cultural wars. The Quebec transformation to modernity is no less dramatic for being largely peaceful. Accompanying dislocations drove the preeminence of the arts—including literature, theater, cinema, television, circus, music, and dance—as a form of bringing together high culture with street performance.[101]

Dance became embedded in Montreal life—a space from which it had been absent—because the dance community constructed a broad range of supporting institutions—ranging from studios and schools to Les Grand Ballets Canadiens, Le Ballet Jazz de Montréal, the dance programs at l'UQÀM and Concordia, provincial and federal arts programs, and arts spaces such as l'Agora de la danse—which combined to produce a solid foundation on which artistic talent could take flight. Dance thrived in Montreal because it became rooted in local society by interacting with it.

Each of these components allowed this once-disparaged art form to attain pride of place in a single lifetime. They precisely produced the resplendent anarchy that Françoise Sullivan and the other petitioner-signers of *Le Refus Global* extolled as a primal source of creativity. Or, as Sullivan herself would note four decades later in a 1988 address at Toronto's York University, "Art can only flourish if it grows from problems which concern the age and is always pushed in the direction of the unknown. Hence, the marvelous in it." [102]

These essentials—and the visionaries who created them—similarly prepared Montreal dance for the trials of the century to follow. With dozens of dance schools and hundreds of dancers, the world of twenty-first century dance in Montreal is highly organized, complex, and dynamic. Opportunities exist from studios for children just discovering dance to internationally recognized and celebrated companies, choreographers, and dancers. From classical, to modern, to avant-garde and experimental, audiences and professionals move back and forth among genres, often interacting with varied subcommunities as they do.

After World War II, pioneers such as the Morenoffs, Gérard Crevier, Françoise Sullivan, and Ludmilla Chiriaeff were viewed as exotics performing in school basements, library halls, gymnasiums, and televisions studios. Now anyone can find his or her place on increasingly specialized stages, secured by deep connections with the world at large.

The story of performance dance in Montreal is deeply connected to the peculiarities of place. The city's linguistic divide favored forms of artistic expression such as dance which transcended language. The arrival of television, still searching for its place in local life, carried dance into living rooms, encouraging a populist dance scene. Dance professionals consequently shunned notions of refined culture that so shaped the reputation of dance in cities that developed their cultural communities previously. The opening to immigrants to meet labor shortages throughout Canada made it possible for many dance professionals to come to the city from abroad.

Performance dance also took root in a city very much divided politically, making all cultural expression forms partisan. Dance, consciously and not, engaged with the political forces unleashed by a new embrace of the modern and by growing demands for sovereignty. The interface between cultural development and politics proved as central in Washington, where nothing escapes partisan interpretation.

Chapter 3

Washington: Experimental Theater in Community Service—The Theater Club Engages Race Relations

The theater enthusiasts Hazel and John Wentworth launched the Washington Theater Club during the late 1950s in a cozy carriage house at 1632 O Street NW. The cottage-sized O Street stage remained the club's signature venue for much of its existence.[103] Located between Dupont and Logan circles, the theater was next to a large church along a short residential block. The building had moved beyond horses, carriages, and automobiles to become a nondescript warehouse. The carriage house offered just enough room for an Elizabethan-style thrust stage surrounded on three sides by 142 seats.

Hazel and John were hungry for innovative drama of a sort absent from Washington at the time. They established their group to promote fresh dramatic forms, to present new ideas, and to support novice playwrights and their work. John Wentworth already had directed the amateur Unitarian Players, and he looked to expand his presence on the city's professional stages. Hazel would assume leadership of the group after the couple's divorce during the 1960s.

The Wentworths further sought to present high-quality productions performed and enjoyed by diverse casts and audiences outside the noisome racial boundaries and Jim Crow customs that still marred the city. They cultivated a slightly Bohemian tone, often presenting nonmainstream works such as poetry readings accompanied by modern dance, tied together with contemporary drama such as Ionescu's *The Lesson*.[104]

The quirkily extravagant Midwesterner Davey Marlin-Jones came from New York to take over as the company's artistic director in 1965.[105] Over the seven years before his 1972 departure, the club mounted some of its most ambitious productions.[106] He generally was well regarded for leveraging his at-times-showy personality to win friends for his theater, and the arts.[107]

In 1968, Marlin-Jones and the company became the first Washingtonians to receive the coveted Margo Jones Award honoring pioneering leaders in American regional theater.[108] Marlin-Jones remained in town as art critic for the CBS-TV affiliate (presently WUSA-TV) until 1987, when he moved to Las Vegas.[109]

An Idea and a Dream

At its height, the Washington Theater Club attracted about 10,000 subscribers, nearly all of whom paid an extra dollar each year to retain membership. For much of its existence, the company offered actor training to children and teens as well as professional training for adults.[110] The club remained dedicated to children's theater, and to promoting puppetry and mime.[111] Its commitment to music ran equally deep. The club's chamber music ensemble—the Theater Chamber Players, founded by Leon Fleisher and Dina Koston in 1968—served long-term residencies at the Smithsonian Institution and the Kennedy Center; and remains active to this day.[112]

Before too long, the diminutive O Street carriage house became "cramped," "uncomfortable," and "confined." "Old as charming" transmuted into "old as dilapidated."[113] Zoning regulations impinged on the club's attempts to grow into a dramatic arts center and school. Such constraints led the club to overextend its financial reserves for a second stage. Meanwhile, the original venue remained much beloved by many; and it continued to serve as a home for children's productions, poetry readings, dance, and music performances as well as puppet theater.[114]

The club, which proudly declared itself for years to be the smallest professional repertoire company in America, looked to expand. When 1969 became 1970, Hazel Wentworth moved primary operations to a remodeled African American church in the city's West End. With three-times the number of seats and plentiful backstage space, the expanded Washington Theater Club suited the company well. A once noteworthy, predominately African

American blue-collar neighborhood, the West End had fallen into disrepair after plans for an inner beltway circling downtown targeted the area for demolition. A neighborhood renewal plan released in 1972 envisioned an upscale urban "new town for the West End."[115] A Ritz Carlton hotel now stands on the site of the Washington Theater Club's final home.

Between 1957 and 1974, the club served as a proving ground for actors starting out their careers, including several who would come to dominate the American stage and screen, such as Ned Beatty, James Broderick, Eleanor Bron, Roscoe Lee Browne, Adolph Caesar, Mary Jo Catlett, John Fortune. Charles Gordone, Micki Grant, Bill Gunn, Gene Hackman, John Hillerman, Yaphet Kotto, Joshua Mostel, Lester Rawlins, and Billy Dee Williams. From the beginning, the club promoted Black theater and Black writers and artists.[116]

Origin Tales

John B. Wentworth seems always to have been a bit at odds with life.[117] He eventually turned to two great passions—theater and activism—to soothe the contradictions churned up by his internal uncertainties. For a while, he did so in partnership with his wife Hazel, who would assume control of his theater company after their divorce.

At first, John banded together with like-minded parishioners at the historic All Souls Unitarian Church to create an ambitious amateur acting group, the Unitarian Players. Such spontaneously formed companies came and went. They peppered a local theater scene bereft of professional theater in the wake of ongoing protests and boycotts over Washington's Jim Crow practices by the nation's leading theatrical figures.

All Souls was—and remains—one of the capital's leading progressive congregations. By the mid–twentieth century, the congregation had long served as a gathering point for the city's progressives. The church pursued its ministry through the arts, hosting racially integrated music groups, leading jazz musicians, and visual artists. Most famously, in 1962, Stan Getz and Charlie Byrd recorded their album *Jazz Samba* in the church's Pierce Hall, introducing Americans to the cool sounds of Brazil.

Wentworth found like-minded, artistically inclined social activists among All Souls parishioners. Background material in the June 3, 1953, program for a production of Philip King's *See How They Run* at Saint George's Episcopal Church Parish Hall tells the story: "The Unitarian Players Group has expanded rapidly from the handful of enthusiasts of 1949 to the proficient and hard-working group of 1953.... Most of us are Unitarians; like to work on shows.... Our programs are aimed at variety—not the show business magazine but the stuff that is the spice of life. Each year, we've mixed comedy with serious drama. Our basic fare has been contemporary, with a seasoning of the so-called 'Classics.' Theater in the Western world got its start from churches.... Live theater offers church people a creative outlet."[118]

Over the course of a decade, the Unitarian Players presented nearly three dozen works, usually in brief, weekend-long runs at various churches and clubs around the region. The shows, for the most part, presented light fare, often with a contemporary bent. Significantly, for what would follow, Wentworth developed a program of memberships and nurtured teenage theater.

Finding a Home and a Voice

Ever more ambitious, John acquired a two-story former carriage house at 1632 O Street NW in January 1957. He and Hazel converted the ground floor into an air-conditioned auditorium with seating on three sides of the stage, a foyer, business offices, rehearsal space, and a prop room. They placed the dressing rooms and additional storage space in the basement while setting the second floor aside for costume storage and their home.[119]

These initial start-up months set a pattern of financial and legal wrangling, which undercut artistic vitality. District authorities, for example, turned them down when the Wentworths applied to the Zoning Board for a variance to operate as a public hall. A follow-on appeal carried the day by noting that the club would operate the theater rather than the Wentworths themselves. The court documents filed by the Wentworths noted that Washington "lags behind other cities such as New York, Cleveland, Pittsburgh, Erie, and others which have fine professional companies, integrated with schools, using local people and playwrights in so far as possible."[120] In the end, the club's educational outreach activities appear to have released the necessary licenses so that, in the summer of 1960, the club could premier its first season.[121]

Despite such legal, administrative, and logistical concerns, the club moved to establish its bone fides as an artistic innovator by holding a playwrighting contest leading to five performances over the course of 1959.[122] Such support for amateur playwriting would continue.[123] Simultaneously, the Wentworths launched workshops for adults and a teen theater. These efforts solidified the club's connection to Washington and helped to raise funds through tuition, fees, and club membership dues.[124]

Having cleared away the bureaucratic, legal, and financial underbrush, the club turned its attention to its artistic agenda. In a handwritten statement from the time of its opening, the club set down a vision for its future: "What is its goal in Washington? To provide professional, legitimate theater setting where the community can come alive with live theater."[125] The time had arrived to put on plays.

Programmatically, the Wentworths were drawn to newer, edgier, and more unconventional theatrical fare than other Washington theaters. For the Wentworths, the new Bohemian Off-Broadway scene taking shape in Lower Manhattan offered a model to follow. Diverse productions drawing on mid-century French playwriting included a notable 1968 production of Albert Camus's *Caligula* featuring John Hillerman in the title role and the African American actor Damon Brazwell.[126]

Shutting Down Jim Crow

Washington's Jim Crow traditions and policies cast a long shadow over the city's theatrical life during the mid–twentieth century.[127] In 1946, Ingrid Bergman and Sam Wanamaker, performing the pre-Broadway tryout of *Joan of Lorraine*, threatened to walk out in protest over the exclusion of African American patrons at George Washington University's new Lisner Auditorium. The show went on as scheduled, so as not to violate contractual obligations, while both Actors' Equity and the Dramatists' Guild began picketing this and other local productions. The next year, national theater leaders declared a boycott of both the National Theater and Lisner Auditorium, triggering a national embargo against the city's professional stages that lasted into the 1950s.

In 1951, Sir John Gielgud agreed to coach young Earl Hyman in a summer production of *Hamlet* on the Howard University campus. Gielgud, Hyman, and director Owen Dodson met at the Greyhound Bus Station, which offered the trio one of the few integrated places to have lunch together.

A few theater notables defied custom and opened up performances to integrated audiences. In 1944, the future Pulitzer Prize–winning critic Walter Kerr, then teaching at Catholic University, integrated both the production and audiences of his patriotic extravaganza celebrating American folks songs, *Sing Out, Sweet Land*. Catholic University's Father Gilbert V. Hartke integrated audiences when he took over management of nearby Olney Summer Theater in Maryland after the war. [128]

Zelda and Thomas Fichandler and Edward Mangum opened Arena Stage to integrated audiences in 1950. By the 1960s, Arena would engage the city's racial divide, eventually bringing African American theater artists to its stage as they presented powerful works examining racial themes beginning in the mid-1960s.[129]

Emerging from the community of activists at All Souls Church, the Wentworths connected their theatrical endeavors to the challenges of race from the beginning. Like the Fichandlers, the Washington Theater Club served integrated audiences from its first performance; and went further.

The Wentworths steadfastly sought to engage Washington's African American community by opening their theaters to jazz concerts and other community events.[130] They did not limit their outreach to the stage, but also engaged Black theater artists and musicians in all aspects of their operations (including bringing the songstress Roberta Flack onto their Board of Directors).[131] In 1963, they invited the African American dancer, choreographer, and

Washington: Experimental Theater

educator Katherine Dunham to join the novelist James T. Farrell to discuss "the repeating cycle of artistic inspiration."[132] In 1972, they hosted benefit performances to support Black theater nationally.[133]

Additionally, African Americans appeared on the Washington Theater Club's stage in plays, lectures, and musical performances. Bill Gunn is the first African American actor in the club's records as having appeared as a cast member. He played in the club's seventh production in 1961, Michael Shurtleff's *Call Me By My Rightful Name*.[134]

Shurtleff's play was "suggested" by Shirley Pfoutz's novel *The Whipping Boy*, about Columbia University roommates Doug, who is white, and Paul, who is Black. A bout of jealousy prompted by the unexpected visit of Doug's brother's girlfriend, Chris, combined with a night of bountiful alcohol consumption to destroy what had been a model relationship between the two roomies.[135]

The play was one of the first performed in Washington to explore the dynamics of interracial relationships in an everyday manner. Shurtleff was a powerhouse in the New York theater world of the era, serving as primary casting director for the producer David Merrick and writing the "casting bible" *Audition*.[136] The noteworthy acting coach Geoffrey Horne played David; and Collin Wilcox, on the eve of her breakout performance as Mayella Violet Ewell in *To Kill A Mockingbird*, was Chris.[137] *Washington Post* critic Richard L. Coe found Gunn's performance "fine."

Gunn was well into a distinguished career as a playwright, novelist, actor, and film director. He would win an Emmy Award a decade later in 1972, he developed a cult following with his 1973 horror film *Ganja and Hess*, and he became a mainstay of the New York arts community throughout the 1970s and 1980s. His appearance in this club production established a pattern of the Wentworths—and, later, Marlin-Jones—providing invaluable opportunities for aspiring African American artists.[138]

Looking Beyond Color Barriers

The Wentworths did not limit Black actors to plays about race relations. In April 1963, the club hosted an integrated touring company from New York, performing various autobiographical writings by Berthold Brecht, *Brecht on Brecht*.[139] More a set of readings than a play, George Tabort's translations of Brecht's musings about himself proved an entertaining evening.[140] So much so, that the club held the play over for several weeks, with its actors popping up at numerous events around town.[141] Cast members included the now-legendary Black actors Roscoe Lee Browne and Micki Grant, together with the notable performers Logan Ramsey and Dolores Sutton. Browne returned in March 1974 to perform in what became the club's final production, *Behind the Broken Word*, in which he paired with the film actor Anthony Zerbe to read contemporary poetry of special meaning to both actors.[142]

In another example of bringing Black actors into the company for plays that were not about racial themes, the club's 1965 production of Shakespeare's *The Tempest* is best known for Lester Rawlins' magisterial turn as Prospero, a performance that passed into Washington theater lore.[143] The *Post*'s Coe heaped individual praise at the time on the newcomer Adolph Caesar's "superbly realized Caliban."[144] Caesar remained part of the club's Resident Company, perfecting the craft that would earn him Academy Award and Golden Globe nominations and several other awards over a celebrated career.[145]

The Wentworths also made their stage available to African American companies performing works of their own. These plays, such as the 1970 production *The Black Experience*, were not affiliated with the club directly. The club's willingness to make its facilities available to Black theater artists (albeit for a fee) helped such works exploring the Black experience to expand the reach of theater in Washington.[146]

These productions reveal a dedication to exploring race relations through theater at a tumultuous moment in the city's history. Such engagement proved even more powerful when the club's productions explicitly focused on the question of race in America, and beyond.

The French playwright Jean Genet's *The Blacks: A Clown Show* was a perfect play for the club. An absurdist satire in which Black actors—some in "white face"—portray the murder trial of a white woman before a kangaroo court, *The Blacks* opened in

Paris in October 1959. It traveled across the Atlantic to a famed off-Broadway production opening at the Saint Mark's Playhouse in May 1961 for a run of over 1,400 performances. The New York show is remembered for the future stars who appeared over the course of its long run, including James Earl Jones, Roscoe Lee Browne, Louis Gossett Jr., Cicely Tyson, Godfrey Cambridge, Raymond St. Jacques, Maya Angelou, and Charles Gordone.[147]

Robert Hooks, writing on the eve of a later production at his DC Black Repertory Company and subsequently at the newly opened Kennedy Center, recalled that, upon seeing the 1961 New York show, he "left the theater completely hypnotized by the powerful statement I had just witnessed. But how, I wondered, could Jean Genet, a white writer, capture so vividly the unique feelings of an oppressed non-white people?" Hooks concluded that Genet was an outcast, whose mental, physical, and artistic shocks gave him "the sensitive and profound insight into our—the Black man's—bitter struggle against worldwide oppression."[148] Robert Hooks' production marked a high-water mark for his DC Black Rep, a company of considerable artistic achievement, which, like the Washington Theater Club, succumbed to Washington's inhospitable financial environment for theater.[149]

Critics found Genet's play "too European." Such "European-ness" would have been a recommendation to the Wentworths. Directed by Gene Frankel, the club's production opened in September 1964, with a cast that included several veterans of the still fresh New York production.[150] Billy Dee Williams joined with Len Scott, Charles Gordone, Nick La Tour, and Adolph Caesar (who was becoming a club regular). The production opened just a handful of weeks after the signing of the Civil Rights Act of 1964, making a powerful statement about the need for Washington theater to engage issues of race relations.

Three months later, the club presented another explosive work examining race relations, this time in South Africa: Artholl Fugard's *The Blood Knot*.[151] Directed by Edmund Cambridge of the Negro Ensemble Company and featuring Yaphet Kotto, who was just starting his extended and illustrious career, the play focused around two half brothers. Both born of an African mother, one brother had a white father, and the other, a Black father, setting up a painful exploration of South Africa's Apartheid regime.

New Director Davey Marlin-Jones jumped right into the topic of race relations upon his arrival in 1965.[152] As the *Post* recorded at the opening of his first season, "Before an audience as classy as its own IQ average, O Street's intimate 145 seat Washington Theater Club opened its sixth professional season with a capable performance of William Hanley's *Slow Dance on a Killing Ground.*"[153]

Hanley's play had premiered in New York a year earlier, creating considerable critical clamor.[154] The story transpires in a rundown Brooklyn candy store as three disparate characters find refuge and share their terrible secrets. An older German immigrant and a young streetwise African American try to calm an anxious young woman who has discovered that she is pregnant. The immigrant's secret is that he had been a victim of German concentration camps; the young Black, that he is on the run; the woman, that she is looking for the address of an illegal abortionist. Their stories unfold as each character circles, threatens, and ultimately discover their shared sadness.

Marlin-Jones chose the work as his first production because it was unknown to Washington audiences, provided an intimate scale suited the club's small stage, and engaged with social concerns.[155] The production brought Billy Dee Williams back to join club stalwarts John Hillerman and Sue Lawless.[156]

The club and Marlin-Jones returned to racial themes two years later at the start of its 1967 season with David Westheimer's *My Sweet Charlie*.[157] The play was an early example of Marlin-Jones bringing a new work unsuccessful in New York to Washington for a new start. In this instance, the gambit worked, as the play would become a made-for-television movie in 1970. The story of a Black who has accidentally murdered a young southern white girl delves into how we can come to live together through dialogue. *Washington Daily News* critic Bob Todd found Damon Brazewell's turn as the Black Charlie superior to the New York original production.[158]

The next fall, Marlin-Jones opened his season with a world premiere of a work—*The Gingham Dog*—destined for Broadway success a year later. A then-unheard-of thirty-year-old playwright—Lanford Wilson—had penned the play as he stood on the verge of untold success.[159] The play was precisely what the Wentworths and Marlin-Jones sought: an important new American work by a previously unknown author interrogating some of the most lethal social issues of the day.

Wilson tells the story of the tortuous break up of an upwardly mobile interracial couple, Vincent and Gloria, who have been living in Harlem. They had grown apart over the course of their three-year-old marriage, with Gloria finding new meaning in her life through Black activism, while Vincent, a liberal white southerner, slipped into disillusionment with his gray-flannel life. Wilson places the action during the tumultuous period, when Vincent decides to move out—a time when mutual recriminations and accusations fly as they divide their possessions.[160]

Critics greatly anticipated the opening and found Robert Darnell and Micki Grant's performances as Gloria and Vincent exceptional.[161] Others saw its Washington premiere as further proof that the center of American theater's creative energy was flowing from New York.[162] Wilson explained to *Post* interviewer John Laurie that the play's title comes from the childhood verse "The Gingham Dog and the Calico Cat" that ends with both eating the other up.[163]

Marlin-Jones returned to issues of race relations later that season with the writer Alexander Panas and William Goldstein's new musical *Mr. Tambo, Mr. Bones*.[164] Panas, an actor and writer best known for his contributions to *Miami Vice* and *Escape from Hell Island*, created a minstrel show taking place within the mind of John Wilkes Booth as he plots to assassinate President Lincoln. Mr. Tambo, a stock minstrel character who plays the tambourine, and Mr. Bones, known for rattling bones, appear in Black and white face. Goldstein set this phantasmagoria to music. John Hillerman played Booth; Bob Spencer, Tambo; and Bryan Clark, Bones.[165] The play received a great deal of press attention—mostly negative—in part because of the importance of Lincoln and his legacy in a city still reeling from the assassination of the Reverend Dr. Martin Luther King just months before.[166]

One additional masterpiece concerning the question of race relations lie ahead. In 1973, the club presented Lonne Elder III's Pulitzer Prize–nominated play about a Harlem barber and his family, *Ceremonies in Dark Old Men*.[167] Elder's play was coming off of a much-praised initial production at New York's Negro Ensemble Company, which opened in 1969 and ran for 320 performances.[168]

Elder became a mainstay of the New York theater scene until his death in 1996.[169]

Elder was the first African American writer to be nominated for an Academy Award for his screenplay for the film *Sounder* just before the play's opening in Washington (Jeremy Larner eventually won for *The Candidate*). Bette Howard, later founder of the prestigious Black Spectrum Theatre Company of Queens (New York), directed the production. Sheila Johnson, later cofounder of BET and the first African American woman to attain a net worth of $1 billion, made her stage debut. Other cast members included William T. Newman Jr. and Frank Adu. Unsurprisingly, given the talent involved, the play was held over, moving from its West End location to the O Street Playhouse, and it attracted the largest audience in club history for any show (14,500, with over 1,000 unfulfilled ticket orders).[170]

Ceremonies in Dark Old Men brought new American playwriting talent addressing important social issues to an audience that embraced both whites and Blacks. Unfortunately, tax authorities and creditors already were serving the club's death notice. Hazel Wentworth reached out to Paul Allen, founder of the Black American Theater, for support.[171] This gambit bought both Wentworth and Allen some time. Their alliance led to one final spectacular examination of race in America, this time in the form of a musical: Eve Merriam and Helen Miller's *Inner City*.[172]

Inner City was not, strictly speaking, a club production. Instead, Paul Allen's Black American and Ebony Promptu Theater Companies used the house under an agreement with Wentworth. The mimeographed program explains that the production began as a "street cantata" based on Eve Merriam's *Inner City Mother Goose*, which was adapted for Broadway by the director Tom O'Horigan, with music by Helen Miller and lyrics by Merriam.[173] The production was more than a stage rental, as it opened doors to several "what might have beens" if the economics of theater had not worked out differently.

Miller was already a major songwriter with several hits to her name and more to come; Merriam was an accomplished author of children's poetry. The choreographer, George Faison, was on his way to becoming a dance icon. A graduate of Washington's Dunbar

High and Howard University, he began working on Broadway at age twenty-eight.[174] This production included twenty-eight "neighborhood characters" and several musicians and evolved from the first run to the second.

The Wentworth–Allen alliance might have saved both companies if it had been formed earlier.[175] Allen's company grew into the New Theater of Washington and continued the outreach initiatives that had been so important to the Wentworths.[176] He eventually moved into the club's original O Street theater, remaking it as the Paul Robeson Center focusing on community theater.[177]

Curtain Time

Theater as art and theater as activism were always tied closely together in John Wentworth's mind. This connection remained strong throughout the evolution of his and Hazel's theater company from the time it took the All Souls stage as the amateur Unitarian Players until its final performances as a regional theater two decades later. Such unity of purpose combined with John's inherent feistiness to generate conflict with neighbors, local police, and other officials, within the company, and ultimately between him and Hazel.

The Club's popularity connected with other changes taking place in a rapidly growing metropolitan region. An expanding federal government bureaucracy created ever more plentiful positions for highly educated middle-income employees. An increasing number of private sector positions serving that government sector multiplied the base of those who enjoyed reading, watching films, attending plays, with additional dollars to spend on cultural pursuits. Washington became a city of bookstores, independent cinemas and upstart theater companies throughout the 1960s, 1970s, and 1980s. The Washington Theater Club was part of an expanding cultural scene where far more tickets were sold for concerts and theater performances than for sporting events.

Hazel's efforts to keep the troupe alive approached the heroic, particularly after her divorce from John. The club retained ardent fans and munificent donors until the end. Their foes eventually had the final say in the form of a judicial ruling against their repeated petitions for nonprofit status.

The club was not alone in facing grasping tax authorities. The District government and pre–home rule congressional oversight authorities denied performing arts institutions—both for-profit and nonprofit—relief from new taxes imposed on admission to entertainment in all forms at the end of the 1960s. Arts organizations from the National Theater and the National Symphony to Arena Stage and the club protested to no avail. Either they absorbed the new tax or passed it on to their ticket holders.[178]

The club's challenges ran deeper. Having been unable to secure a designation as an educational nonprofit organization, the club became exposed to property tax assessments on quite a different scale from the proposed admission tax. By the early 1970s, the club faced the imposition of real estate taxes on two properties. Those taxes briskly increased, especially for the 23rd Street theater, which stood at the center of a West End neighborhood with rapidly escalating property values.[179]

By 1972, all ways forward rested on the club's ability to secure a tax exemption as an educational nonprofit organization. Absent a definitive decision, Hazel held out diminished but continuing hope that the club would survive. Then, she and the club encountered Judge W. Byron Sorrell, of the Superior Court of the District of Columbia.

For years, the Wentworths had followed Arena Stage's lead in claiming to be an educational not-for-profit. Arena founders Zelda and Thomas Fichandler creatively transformed their company from a commercial theater to an educational nonprofit to secure foundation grants. The Fichandlers' gambit required congressional legislation as well as a fulsome commitment to youth and other educational programs. The Wentworths' case similarly rested on their long-standing and active programs engaging the Washington area's youth.

In September 1972, Judge Sorrell ruled that the club had failed to justify an exemption from real estate taxes for its 23rd and L Street location.[180] The court instructed the club to pay $30,000 in back taxes and interest to the District covering the period July 1970 through June 1973.[181] Subsequent appeals, and an effort to push legislative remedy through Congress to protect the club, failed.[182]

The story of the Washington Theater Club is one of missed opportunities. The story similarly is one of great achievement, creating a theater of high artistic standards that engaged the leading challenges facing its community. From bringing new works to the American stage to focusing on African American authors, artists, and works, the Wentworths, Davey Marlin-Jones, and everyone else associated with the Washington Theater Club created a legacy worthy of notice.

Washington was not alone in coming of age culturally during this era. Toronto, spurred on to an equally dramatic expansion of its economy and opportunities for educated professionals, embraced theater as a means for expressing its growing cultural ambitions. Provoked in part by a Quebec sovereigntist movement that questioned the city's cultural distinctiveness from the United States, Toronto theater-makers began to exclaim their distinctive presence.

Chapter 4

Toronto in the 1970s as 1920s Paris: Imagining a National Identity from the Stage

James Kaplan once wrote in *The New Yorker* that "Toronto in 1972 resembled one of those artistic nexuses that crop up now and then, like Paris in the twenties, Los Angeles in the thirties, London just before the First World War."[183] Kaplan may have engaged in hyperbole, yet he was correct that Torontonians and the newcomers arriving there found life full of artistic surprises and innovations.

Many have speculated that New York became a mecca of creativity during the 1960s and 1970s because it was dangerous, dirty, and cheap. Artists could afford to live in Lower Manhattan and have the place to themselves because no one else wanted to be there. Pregentrification Toronto was safe, reasonably clean, and cheap. No one feared coming home late from a surprise show by the Rolling Stones at the El Mocambo on Spadina, a recital by the visiting Soviet cellist Mstislav Rastropovich at the acoustically stunning Massey Hall downtown, or a ballet performance at Saint Lawrence Hall with the recent defector Mikhail Baryshnikov. Students could afford to catch Gilda Ratner and Dan Aykroyd at Second City downtown, or Joni Mitchell and Gordon Lightfoot at a cellar club in Yorkville.

Someone dropping into the cheap eateries along Bloor Street West between Saint George and Bathurst—be they burger joints or the ubiquitous family-run Magyar restaurants that sprang up after the failed 1956 Hungarian Revolution—would have overheard heated conversations about the latest lectures by Alan Bloom on Plato, Northrop Frye on Canadian identity, or Marshall McLuhan on the electronic future. Some speculated about the recordings

Glenn Gould undoubtedly was making in the auditorium of Eaton's Department Store near the intersection of College and Yonge streets. American cultural imperialism, Quebec separatism, and Pierre Elliott Trudeau's latest family saga were also sure to dominate.

Perhaps an evening of beer and Dixieland Jazz might follow at the century-old Brunswick House Pub. Many denizens of these haunts returned to the nearby University of Toronto Saint George Campus, or melted into the as-yet-Bohemian Annex neighborhood that had become home to grad students, professors, and trendy intellectuals such as the urbanist Jane Jacobs, the environmentalist David Suzuki, and the writer Margaret Atwood.

Supercharged by the 1967 Canadian Confederation Centennial celebrations, Toronto intellectuals of all stripes pondered what it meant to be Canadian.[184] The answer was hardly simple. Challenged by growing Quebec nationalism for being American wannabes, English Canadians struggled with a self-definition that was neither American nor colonial British. The quest for distinctiveness stoked all the arts, but none more than creative writing.

In 1931, there were little more than 3,000 writers and journalists in the entire country, or one for every 3,100 Canadians. Then the number of those who earned a living from words exploded during the 1960s and 1970s, so that nearly 15,000 Canadians (or one in 1,500) worked as writers, editors, and journalists by 1970 (that number would reach 50,000—or 1 in roughly 600—by the twenty-first century).[185]

Creating a Literary Canon

These writers did what writers do; they wrote. By 1970, a tidal wave of Canadian-themed book publishing swept the country.[186] Arguably the first specialized university courses in "CanLit" began at Toronto's York University in 1973. Every Canadian university—and nearly every high school—added courses on Canadian literature to their curricula by decade's end.[187] Their syllabi focused on a remarkable flowering of poetry and prose by such writers as Margaret Atwood, Leonard Cohen, Mavis Gallant, Alice Munro,

Michael Ondaatje, Mordecai Richler, and Michel Tremblay, to name but a few. A national literary canon came into being. For English-speaking Canadians, this scene focused on Toronto.

These changes came about in part because earmarked federal and provincial cultural policies promoted "Canadian content." In April 1949, Prime Minister Louis St.-Laurent appointed what became known as the "Massey Commission" to investigate the state of the arts and culture in Canada. Vincent Massey, a future governor general of Canada and brother of actor Raymond Massey, chaired the formally titled Royal Commission on National Development in the Arts, Letters, and Sciences. Massey and his commissioners traveled across the country, holding 114 meetings in 16 Canadian cities and hearing testimony from more than 1,200 witnesses.

The commission's 1951 report found that Canadian cultural institutions were imperiled by the country's vast distances, scattered population, and growing dependence on the United States. Many of its recommendations came to fruition, including enhanced funding for government-supported broadcasting, Canadian content restrictions on media, the establishment of a national library and archives, and the creation of a national gallery of art.

The federal government followed the Massey Commission's recommendations by launching a new funding agency dedicated to the arts, the humanities, and social science: the Canada Council. By the 1960s, Toronto writers, artists, and their institutional partners were receiving meaningful support from various federal and provincial funding agencies.[188]

Increasing government involvement in arts funding complemented the coming of age of the most economically confident generation in Canadian history. Canada's postwar Baby Boomers grew up with unprecedented opportunities for personal development. Economic security followed into late adolescence as the Canadian university system entered an era of unmatched expansion. University education became a distinction shared by tens of thousands of young Canadians whose parents never enjoyed similar opportunities. The ability to spend a few years knocking around a university campus, a Bohemian urban enclave, or a creative profession fell within the reach of more Canadians than ever before; including some with genuine talent and insight into the human condition. Culture was no longer elsewhere.

Modern English Canadian poetry emerged in Montreal during the 1920s and 1930s, as poets such as A. J. M. Smith, F. R. Scott, A. M. Klein, P. K. Page, and Louis Dudek drew sustenance from their city's cosmopolitan diversity.[189] By the 1950s, a Toronto newly freed from some of the most restrictive liquor laws on the continent began to develop a colorful arts scene of its own. Tens of thousands arriving immigrants from societies where culture mattered further fed this trend. Simultaneously, the English-language literary scene in Montreal faltered in the face of a rising Francophone nationalist challenge (although writers such as Mordecai Richler and Leonard Cohen ensured that Montreal remained an important hub of Canada's English-language literary culture).

Meanwhile, clubs in Toronto's growing Yorkville scene, such as the Embassy, picked up the slack. Drawing student audiences from the University of Toronto's Saint George Campus, club owners started offering a smorgasbord of cultural offerings, from folk music and jazz on weekends to poetry readings on weeknights. This Yorkville scene did not survive the neighborhood's tourist celebrity by the end of the decade.[190] But Toronto's literary and art scenes began to hold their own before Montreal's.

Newly established Rochdale College on the opposite side of the university campus became a cultural hatchery of another sort. Built as a Brutalist eighteen-story concrete residence hall for university students, Rochdale opened in 1968 as a student-run experiment in alternative education and cooperative living. In theory, up to 840 resident faculty and students would live together in what was at the time the largest co-op residence on the continent. Complex subsidized rent plans soon collapsed under lax management and its tuition-free informal educational track never came together (although Rochdale master's degrees were available for $50 and doctorates for $100). At one point, the co-op hired biker clubs to provide security. The building became a hotbed of radical politics and drugs, dramatized by periodic police raids, before this failed experiment in communal living shut down for good in 1975. Rochdale eventually became subsidized housing for senior citizens.[191]

For all its troubles—and, in part, because of them—Rochdale became an important incubator for several cultural institutions that proved to be central to the city's creative success, including Coach

House Press, House of Anansi Press, Theatre Passe Muraille, and the Toronto Free Dance Theatre. Its idealistic, artsy atmosphere and free-care attitude toward rent made Rochdale a model launching pad for small-scale cultural entrepreneurs.

Modest independent publishers came and went during the 1960s, as their significance at times outweighed their longevity. For example, Margaret Atwood self-published her first collection of verse—*The Circle Game*—with diminutive Contact Press in 1966. Its origins did not undermine the volume's significance, as it won the young writer the Governor General's Award (Canada's highest literary award) for poetry. Atwood's career was launched with her first novel—*The Edible Woman*—following in 1969 from the established publisher McClelland and Stuart.[192] Coach House Press and the House of Anasi Press emerged from their Rochdale origins to play particularly noteworthy roles in the growth of Canadian literature.

Coach House's founder, the typesetter Stan Bevington, lived on the top floor of Rochdale when he arrived in Toronto from Edmonton. He installed a vintage printing press in a coach house tucked in the alley behind Rochdale (now named for poet bpNichol) and began printing art books and literature by young writers living nearby. The press's early imprint proclaimed that its books were "Printed in Canada by Mindless Acid Freaks." Coach House eventually brought out early works by some of Canada's most illustrious writers, including Atwood, Michael Ondaatje, Anne-Marie MacDonald, George Bowering, Gwendolyn MacEwen, bpNichol, and Anne Michaels. The press, which split into two separate businesses in 1991, also became known for its innovations in printing and in the use of digital technology.[193]

A Rochdale "resource person," the poet Dennis Lee, and the novelist Dave Godfrey founded House of Anansi Press in 1967 to publish works by their friends and colleagues. Named after the trickster of West African folklore, House of Anasi continues to be a significant publisher of Canadian literature.[194] Lee and Godfrey's friends included Atwood, Ondaatje, and Northrop Frye, as well as the French-language authors Anne Hébert, Lise Bissonnette, and Marie-Clair Blais, whose work they printed in English translation. In 1972, the press published Atwood's landmark critical guide to

Canadian literature, *Survival*, in which she identified the concept of "survival" as a distinguishing theme of both French and English Canadian literature. For Atwood, this preoccupation was as central to Canadian literary identity as the notion of "island" was to British literature, and the "frontier" to American literature.[195] *Survival* became a foundational work in the emerging field of CanLit and continues to be read and used in courses today.

Simultaneously, the city emerged as a center for alternative theater exploring Canadian themes.[196] As the Rochdale College story reveals, many leading lights in the new theater scene were part of the same community as those writers exploring Canadian identity through literature. The local worlds of the printed word and the spoken word would remain deeply connected for years to come.

Strutting on Stage

Unlike writers such as Atwood, Toronto's playwrights, directors, producers, and actors faced greater prejudice as they sought to move beyond the local, regional scene. In a remarkably offensive 1973 review appearing in the *New York Times* of a Canadian play, for example, Julius Novick wrote, "'Canadian playwright.' These words seem a little incongruous, like 'Panamanian hockey-player,' almost, or 'Lebanese fur trapper.' But Canadians are now paying more attention than ever before to the question of what it means to be Canadian. A new 'cultural nationalism' is being felt and expressed, and young Canadian playwrights have begun to appear."[197] It would not take long before such an opinion would be seen as arrogant, prejudicial bunkum.

As with literature, Toronto's theater world was transformed during the late 1960s and early 1970s. Some pioneers found inspiration in the daring productions of London's "fringe" playhouses and New York's "off-off Broadway" scene, infused with the era's antiestablishment commotion. As Denis W. Johnston drolly noted, "inexorably, the Toronto public began to perceive theatre as an activity which took place in converted warehouses."[198] The upstart Toronto theaters followed a distinctive path as heightened Canadian patriotism released by the 1967 Centennial celebrations made pursuit of a nationalist program a prerequisite for funding and acceptance. This initial radical outburst ran its course by mid-decade with several originators of Toronto nonmainstream theater scene moving on, leaving a rich legacy of plays, actors, designers, playwrights, and theaters to carry on.[199]

Johnston set out this story in his 1991 account of the rise of Toronto's alternative theaters, *Up the Mainstream*. "Between 1968 and 1972," he writes, "a small group of small theatre companies in Toronto completely changed the way Canadians thought about theatre. Before 1968, before this flood of new theatres and new plays, there was no such thing as an alternative theatre movement in Canada. By 1972, ... the alternative theatres had grown to dominate the theatrical landscape of Canada's largest theatre market and were on the brink of attaining a national influence. The landscape had changed so quickly that the new theatres had not even acquired and agreed-upon name—underground? alternate? alternative? It had changed so thoroughly that, in the minds of Toronto's own intellectual and artistic community, mainstream theatre became little more than an appendance to the alternative."[200]

Numerous changes in the city facilitated this shift. The beginnings of deindustrialization freed up unused warehouses and proletarian neighborhoods for aspiring artists to roost. The city's major daily newspapers—the *Globe and Mail* and *The Star*—competed for recognition as intellectual leaders with the *Globe*'s lead theater critic, Herbert Whittaker, squaring off against the legendary Nathan Cohen at *The Star* until Cohen's death in 1971. The Estonian-Canadian Urjo Kareda, who replaced Cohen, emerged as an articulate voice advocating for Canadian plays and films. Newly arriving Torontonians from around the world included many migrants for whom the arts were central to urban life. Canadians, in turn, looked to the arts to define an emergent identity that withstood the cultural, intellectual, and economic storm sweeping in from the south.

Four theaters dominated this rising scene leading up to 1975: Theatre Passe Muraille, the Factory Theatre Lab, Tarragon Theatre, and Toronto Free Theatre. Several other smaller companies of note passed into and out of existence as well, often exhausted by the constant hunt for secure funding in the face of rising costs and the unending struggle to sustain a distinctive artistic image. Their stories originate with Theatre Passe Muraille and, once again, Rochdale College.

Theatre Passe Muraille

Jim Garrard launched his Theatre Passe Muraille (Theater Beyond Walls) in Rochdale in 1968 as a communal improvisational effort. Garrard and his collaborators intended to create a distinctly Canadian theater that would transcend real estate and the other incumbrances of formal theaters. They made plays up as they went along, moving from Rochdale common rooms to barns, churches, bars, basements, lofts, and streetcars.[201]

Garrard had grown up in rural Ontario too poor to attend a university. After a stint at a local teachers' college, he enrolled in correspondence and summer courses at Queen's University in Kingston, Ontario. He joined in university theatrical productions and eventually completed his undergraduate degree in English, drama, and philosophy. He applied for the acting program at the London Academy of Music and Dramatic Art, was accepted, and headed off to England in 1966. He used his time in London to explore British and French experimental theater and stopped off in New York to see performances at La Mama Experimental Theatre Club. Back in Toronto by February 1968, Garrard was looking for a place to land. He ended up at Rochdale.

Garrard founded Theatre Passe Muraille as Rochdale's Performing Unit, with a resident company of nine actors plus a scattering of other technical specialists. He worked out of a "collapsible, transportable 'plastic theatre'" on Rochdale's second-floor terrace, eventually moving into the college's eighteenth-floor "Zeus Suite." Performances took place in the Rochdale garage.

Along the way, the company presented the American playwright Rochelle Owens's play *Futz*, about a farmer who falls in love with a pig. The play, which first was produced in Minneapolis in 1965, revolves around the farmer Cyrus Futz, who lives with his pet sow Amanda in quiet sin somewhere in the Ozarks. The play gained notoriety in New York and London for bestiality and nudity (Cyrus and Amanda make loud love off stage), before making it to Toronto under Garrard's direction in 1969.[202]

Plainclothes police officers attended opening night at the Central Library Theater, prompted in part by salacious press coverage in the *Toronto Star*. After the actors left by a fire escape to avoid the police, the morality squad appeared the next day with summonses issued to all involved, down to the stage crew and hat-check-boy at the Central Library. The ensuing scandal prompted an avalanche of ticket sales and ongoing debates across Toronto about morality and theater. Eventually, charges were dropped against all except Garrard and three producers. They were initially found guilty of staging an indecent performance but were acquitted on appeal in April 1970.

Everyone who read a Toronto newspaper knew about Garrard's theater. The press tended to portray the defendants as victims of an overzealous police force and an old-fashioned judge. *Futz* was part of a changing scene in Toronto, where strip clubs and social revolution disrupted the city's long-standing reputation as "Toronto the Good." Before too long, a celebrated local production of *Hair* would end all pretense on the part of the moral guardians to return to days past.[203]

The *Futz* controversy understandably wore Garrard down. Faced with unending financial travails—only temporarily offset by a successful double bill of Terrence McNally's *Sweet Eros* and Jon Lennon's *In His Own Words*—he stepped aside, passing leadership first to Martin Kinch, who soon left to found the Toronto Free Theatre with John Palmer and Tom Hendry. Within a year, Paul Thompson inherited the theater's directorship and led the company's legendary run throughout the 1970s.[204]

Thompson initially had a company with neither scripts nor funds. He transformed the theater's production process into a "collective creation" inspired by Montreal's improvisational Theatre d'Audjourd'hui. At first, a group of actors sat down together and tossed around ideas for shows, which they gradually transformed into on-the-fly performances. These efforts took on new meaning when, in 1972, Thompson set out with a group of actors into southwest Ontario farmland, where they worked on the land and got to know local farmers and their communities.

These adventures eventually produced *The Farm Show*, perhaps the most influential work of the Thompson era. Six rural characters—

three men and three women—appeared on a stage with no lights, sets, or seating, except for bales of hay, and told stories, performed impromptu skits, and did songs and dances. Audiences wherever the show went—the show traveled around Ontario, then Canada and the United States, and finally went to England in 1979—loved the simplicity, which seemed to reveal the essence of community and Canadianism.[205]

By 1973, Thompson had launched his "seed-show" program designed to elicit new ideas and scripts based on inviting 5-minute "pitches" to all comers who wanted to see their works on stage.[206] The company focused increasingly on Canadian works and themes, such as the historical plays *1837* about that year's failed rebellion against colonial authority; *William Lyon Mackenzie*, about the country's first prime minister; and, *Maggie and Pierre* about the ongoing soap opera lives of the country's current leading couple, the Trudeaus.[207] The company had a good run performing at Trinity Square, expanding into actor's training and children's theater. That era came to an end when the Church of the Holy Trinity fell within the footprint of the massive Eaton Center shopping mall, which began construction in the early 1970s.

Thompson continued to court controversy. His production of *I Love You, Baby Blue*, celebrating a Friday midnight Toronto cable soft-porn show *Baby Blue*, brought back the morals squad.[208] A judge threw the charges out of court, this time for the absence of evidence of moral turpitude. Toronto had come a long way since its days as a Protestant bastion. The positive side of this evolution for theaters was that directors no longer had to look out at the audience trying to spot agents lurking about the lobby and auditorium. On the other hand, they had an increasingly difficult time generating the sorts of scandals that brought them full halls and coffers.

I Love You, Baby Blue proved a popular and financial success, attracting over 26,000 ticket holders before the police were able to shut it down. These funds contributed to the theater's ability to buy a permanent home in a bakery dating from 1902.

After Thompson's departure in 1981, and secure in an upgraded home theater fully renovated in 1983, Theatre Passe Muraille evolved into a more formal yet innovative house showcasing new Canadian works. The award-winning company has continued to present important theater under more than a half-dozen successful artistic directors. It has retained its reputation combining rebelliousness and nationalism. This distinct brand among the city's theaters—though distinctly muted—dates from its renegade days at Rochdale. Simultaneously, the company has been adept at catching ever-new trends in audience taste. Its story is the story of the new Toronto urban culture taking root.

The Factory Theatre Lab

Ken Gass became enamored of the theater growing up in British Columbia. Having graduated from UBC and feeling confined by a then-stodgy Vancouver, he landed in Toronto in 1968. He earned an Ontario teaching certificate and started teaching high school English at Parkdale Collegiate. Meanwhile, he jumped into the Toronto theater scene, writing theater reviews and eventually connecting with the playwright John Herbert as well as the circles that had grown up around Theatre Passe Muraille and Rochdale. In early 1970, he joined with the artist Frank Trotz to rent the second-floor warehouse above an auto-body shop at 374 Dupont Street and launched the Factory Theatre Lab with an eye toward replicating the New York off-off-Broadway scene.[209]

The rough-and-ready stage connected with a grassroots theater movement, holding workshops for playwrights and new scripts and staging new works. Gass, in an effort to develop a unique brand, declared that the Factory would only produce works by Canadian authors, eventually adding the tagline "the home of the Canadian playwright." He attracted many young Canadian theater professionals returning home from time in British and American theaters and universities, including the director Eric Stener, the director and actor Paul Bettis, the writer George F. Walker, and the administrator Ralph Zimmerman. Bill Glassco was involved during these formative years as well.[210]

The Factory's first major success came in early 1971 with a hit double bill featuring Michael Mirolla's *Snails* and David Freeman's *Creeps* directed by Glassco. Freeman's play would go on to success in New York and elsewhere. Freeman suffered from cerebral palsy and wrote the play set in a workshop for palsy patients. The play's ripping humor immediately attracted critical and audience acclaim (and subsequently numerous awards). The initial three-week run was extended to four, with the Factory's theater selling out for every performance.[211]

Another hit, Louis Capson's *I Love You Billy Striker*, followed. During the Factory's first sixteen months, Gass mounted ten major performances and thirty playwrights' workshops on a budget of $20,000.[212]

Then Gass's stinginess (or, more likely, penury) caught up with him. Canadian Actor's Equity demanded higher compensation for its members. The Factory avoided being shut down only with the support of the broader Toronto theater community. Gass was not so lucky with city fire and safety inspectors, who barred performances in the crude second-floor warehouse. Moreover, the company's operating charter defined its mission as a drama school rather than a performance center. Another battle with municipal assessors ensued.

After a successful British tour during the summer 1973, the company relocated in 1974 to the old Second City space on Adelaide Street downtown.[213] The company moved to its current home—the 1869 Queen Anne Gothic Muley House, with a 1910 addition—in 1983.

Gass and the Lab continued to develop new Canadian works, but the artistic and logistical pressures began to take a toll. The Lab's best known and most controversial work—Gass's own play *Winter Offensive*—premiered in 1977. The work explored the social amorality of Nazi Germany. Its pervasive sex and violence caused audience members to walk out and generated strongly negative reviews and calls for the production to be banned. Gass left the company two years later, and he founded the Canadian Rep Theatre in 1985.[214]

Gass returned as artistic director in 1997 to save the theater from financial collapse. He enjoyed a successful run with several new Canadian works, including, in 1999, the Canadian mathematician John Mighton's award winning *A Short History of Night*. Mighton's play charts the origins of contemporary science through the work of the Danish astronomer Tycho Brahe and the German mystic and astronomer Johannes Kepler as they try to unlock the secrets of the cosmos against the backdrop of sixteenth-century religious wars, witch hunts, and general social mayhem.[215]

Gass fell into a dispute with the Factory's Board of Directors over renovations of the theater's historic venue. The Board, against widespread protest among the Toronto drama community, fired Gass in 2012. The Factory continued to produce new Canadian works. Gass resurrected the Canadian Rep Theater, which continued to produce new works. The Canadian Rep came back to life in 2023 after a COVID-19-imposed hiatus.[216]

The Tarragon Theatre

Bill Glassco came to the Toronto theater scene from a more prominent starting point than some of the crowd hanging around Rochdale. Born in Quebec City to the family of a prominent business executive, he was raised in Toronto's tony Forest Hill neighborhood, attending posh private schools before earning a degree in English from Princeton and a master's from Oxford. Back in Canada, he worked toward a PhD in English at the University of Toronto, lecturing to students along the way.[217]

Bored with his studies and his students, Glassco leveraged family connections to move into the growing local theater scene during the mid-1960s and, upon completing his doctorate, latched onto an administrative position at the Stratford Shakespeare Festival. Eventually, he made his way to New York University, where he studied with Olympia Dukakis and Peter Kass.[218]

Back at his old teaching position at the University of Toronto's Victoria College, Glassco reached out to his family's connections in the Canadian business elite for financial support. He and his wife Jane ran a successful summer stock company—the Red Barn Theatre—in the Ontario cottage country town of Jackson's Pass. They were ready for more.[219]

Glassco connected with Gass's new Factory Theatre Lab, drawn in part by the company's commitment to producing Canadian drama. He gained kudos for his direction of the company's first stage success, *Creeps*, yet wanted a greater opportunity to polish the show in ways the Factory Lab's scanty finances could not support. Bill and Jane found an old warehouse less than two blocks from the Factory Lab, though on the opposite side of very active crosstown freight railroad tracks. Tarragon, with numerous renovations and expansions, has remained at this site ever since.[220]

The Glasscos ran their new Tarragon Theatre as their own, though they recruited several more experienced professionals to join them. Among the newcomers was Bernie Bomers, who had been the business manager of Rochdale College, and who assumed responsibility for the company's financial management. As Johnston explains, "the name 'Tarragon' was a reaction against the kind of alternative theatre which promised half-realized artistic experiments. Instead, it offered the imagery of the kitchen: a bright, comfortable workplace where carefully chosen ingredients are skillfully combined to bring pleasure to one's guests. It also suggested the well-bred courtesy of the Glasscos' upbringing, of a style not to be found at Pass Muraille or the Factory."[221] Tarragon launched in late 1971 with an upgraded production of *Creeps* featuring the same lead actors and elevated production values.

Tarragon quickly secured its reputation as a house promoting homegrown Canadian works. More significantly, it showcased radical French-language plays coming out of the politically intense Montreal scene, most particularly the plays of Quebec theater's bad boy Michel Tremblay.[222]

Tremblay demolished all notions of respectability in French Canadian letters. A child of working-class French speaking Montreal who was raised by a gaggle of women relatives, Tremblay mobilized his wicked wit and ear for unique language to tell stories about those who were invisible to conventional society. As noted above, his first play *Les Belles-Soeurs*, written in the local blue-collar jargon *joual* mixing grammatically incorrect French with English slang, scandalized critics and audiences alike (until his plays won acceptance in Paris, where audiences condescendingly found his lingo charming). His later works continued a focus on the excluded, including many novels and plays that center on gay characters. His appearance at the same moment when Quebec separatism was gaining traction lent political brio to the reception of his writings among French and English Canadians alike.[223]

Glassco discovered Tremblay's work through John Van Burek, who directed a French-language theater group in Toronto, Le Théâtre du P'tit Bonheur. Together, they convinced Tremblay to let them produce their translation of *A Toi, pour tourjours, ta Marie-Lou*. This became the first of a half-dozen Tremblay works that Glassco brought to Toronto audiences for the first time between 1972 and 1988. Meanwhile, Toronto Arts Production mounted Glassco and Van Burek's translation of the seminal *Les Belles Soeurs* for English Canadian audiences in 1973.[224]

Perhaps the most celebrated Canadian production of the decade, Glassco's 1974 production of Tremblay's *Hosanna* set a new standard for Canadian theater.[225] Glassco succeeded in convincing the classical actor Richard Monette to play the lead role of a Montreal transvestite who, dressed as Elizabeth Taylor in the film *Cleopatra*, reexamines her life after having been humiliated at a gay Halloween party.[226] The play ran for an unprecedented seven weeks at Tarragon before moving to the Global Village Theater and on to a three-week run on Broadway.

After producing two dozen Canadian plays during its first four season, Glassco and the other company leaders needed a break. The company was well positioned financially and made its facilities open to other companies during the 1975–76 season. The Glasscos' marriage was less secure and dissolved during this hiatus, ensuring that Tarragon would be somehow different after its return.[227]

After his sabbatical, Tarragon became known for stellar productions of Canadian, American, and international classics. Michel Tremblay and Roland Lepage found their works appearing in the same season as classics by Chekhov, Strindberg, and Brecht/Weill. Its audience became more traditional and its aesthetics more conservative. The company remained a feeder for new Canadian plays to regional theaters around the country. Its days as "alternative" were over, as Glassco found himself running what had become a flagship company among Toronto's mainstream theaters.[228]

In 1981, *Toronto Star* critic Urjo Kareda wrote a conspicuous article in *Toronto Life* magazine titled "Dormant Stage," in which he grumbled that the Toronto theater scene was languishing past its prime. Glassco invited Kareda to lunch to discuss the piece, a tete-à-tete that ended with Glassco offering Kareda the artistic directorship of Tarragon. Kareda accepted. Glassco moved to the new CentreStage company, which, as discussed below, merged with the Toronto Free Theatre in 1988 to form Canadian Stage.[229]

Kareda remained at Tarragon from 1982 until his death in 2001. For two decades, he appeared as one of English Canadian theater's major leaders. He directed productions infrequently. Rather, he used his leadership of Tarragon, and with the affiliated Tarragon Playwrights Unit, to foster new scripts and their authors. His efforts' cumulative impact influenced the direction of English Canadian theater and made him a gatekeeper to what made it onto stages across Canada.

Remarkably, Kareda reviewed up to 500 new scripts per year, and he responded with (in)famously honest and detailed letters. Generally supportive of white, male, Canadian writers, his correspondence—which has been published in the Jessica Riley edited compilation *A Man of Letters*—reveals Kareda to have been more prejudicial toward scripts submitted by Native Canadians, women, Canadians of color, and sexual minorities.[230] These preferences shaped Tarragon's position as ever more establishmentarian as time passed.

Subsequent artistic directors Richard Rose and Mike Payette have leveraged the company's persisting elevated reputation to develop new works while cultivating new audiences and embracing diversity. As the post-COVID version of its website proclaims: "Welcome to Canada's neighborhood theatre. Join us for the next great Canadian play, or explore everything educational from programs, courses, audience resources and going beyond the stage."[231] This mission is perhaps distant from the frisson-producing radical Québécois plays of the 1970s; but it is honorable nonetheless.

The Toronto Free Theatre

John Palmer, Martin Kinch, and Tom Hendry had some history together by the time they set out from Theatre Passe Muraille to launch their own company in 1970. Palmer had grown up in Ottawa, where, after some false starts, he settled into Carleton University's theater program. His school productions won praise and awards, which only grew after he and some of his Carleton mates began performing at the capital's renowned Le Hibou coffee house as the New Vic Theatre.[232] The company captured the attention of theater notables—though not many audience members—during a run alongside the 1967 Stratford (Ontario) Shakespeare Festival. The nearby Shaw Festival at Niagara-on-the-Lake invited the company over for a show on an off day.

That summer's notoriety helped Palmer win a grant to apprentice in Glasgow the next season, after which he came back to Canada for a disastrous summer festival production in Kelowna, Ontario. Returning to Toronto to lick his creative wounds, he sought out Kinch, whom he had met at a university theater festival in Montreal.[233] Kinch was already set up at Rochdale and welcomed his friend to the city's burgeoning alternative theater scene.

The next summer, Palmer and Kinch formed a new company, Canadian Place Theatre, and set up shop in a vacant dry goods store across from the Stratford Festival's Avon Theatre.[234] They befriended the festival's literary manager, Tom Hendry, along the way. After a summer season of mixed reviews, the trio headed back to Toronto, where the Theatre Pass Muraille founder Garrard was promoting Kinch as a company director. Kinch, Palmer, and Hendry would set out in 1970 to form the Free Theatre with the goal of showcasing Canadian works.

The Free, as it would be known, embraced two concepts of freedom. One, creative freedom, matched a theatrical agenda that today would fit under the rubric of "social justice." Two, literally free, as in no admission charge. The hope was that both forms of free would support the other.[235] Idealistic notions of forming a stable cast and opening theater doors to all comers soon collided with the realities of running a theater. Government grants, it turned out, could only go so far.

Palmer headed to New York, Hendley to other projects. Both returned from time to time for specific productions. In fairly short order, the Free had become Kinch's to run.[236] Kinch's love of decadence and gore earned him the sobriquet "Mr. Sex and Violence," a moniker that became attached to the Free as a whole. As Denis W. Johnston puts it, the Free became the type of theater where adolescents would take their parents to gross them out.[237]

Kinch, meanwhile had other projects of his own, such as the highly successful 1971 production of Michael Ondaatje's *The Collective Work of Billy the Kid* at the Saint Lawrence Centre.[238]

The Free launched in 1972, performing initially at the University of Toronto's Hart House Theatre before moving to an 1880s gasworks on Berkeley Street. The Consumers Gas Company abandoned the building in 1955, after which it stood vacant until demolition contractors were hired to tear it down. The contractors fell in love with the building's intricate Victorian brickwork and pleaded for the building to be saved. Serendipity, fate, and theatrical magic came together in 1972 to bring the owners, the contractors, and the Free together. The company created a ninety-nine-seat auditorium and moved in.[239]

Free remained special among the major unconventional theaters at the time. As Johnston writes, "Toronto Free Theatre was the first alternative theatre to be born fully grown. It had paid staff, paid actors, and its own theatre space. Its directors were not neophytes struggling for first recognition but were highly experienced professionals. For these reasons, as well as for the noteworthy innovations of free admission and a resident acting company, the critics treated TFT's first productions as events of some significance."[240]

The Free led off its inaugural season with Hendry's *How Are Things with the Walking Wounded?* set at a cocktail gathering during Montreal's Expo '67 celebrating a gay couple's first anniversary. The critic Urjo Kareda described the script as "Little Orphan Annie meets the Munsters." Other critics and patrons were more forgiving and eagerly waited to see what the Free would perform next.[241] The season ended with Carol Bolt's historical musical *Gabe* featuring giant puppets telling the story of nineteenth-century Métis leaders Louis Riel and Gabriel Dumont (historical figures well known to Canadian school students).[242] The Free was off to a smashing start, with more than 17,000 patrons attending a half-dozen productions in the company's ninety-nine-seat theater.[243]

Over time, the company became synonymous with Kinch's realistic violence and sexuality. The director believed that such portrayals demonstrated the brutality inflicted on society's powerless. Others saw it as gratuitous. The police morality squad issued summonses against the company's 1973 production of *Clear Light* for nudity, a charge that fell through the cracks of the authorities' lackadaisical enforcement.[244] The 1973–74 season featured political works, such as Marc Gélinas's documentary play about the Québécois radical Pierre Vallières (*Vallières!*) and Carol Bolt's musical biography of the anarchist Emma Goldman (*Red Emma*).[245]

Creative enervation and ennui set in after Herculean efforts to launch a theater that was "free" in so many ways. The company shut down for major renovations in May 1976 after four years of stirring Toronto's theatrical pot. The theater reopened nine months later with two stages in the Berkeley Street gasworks to fill. A renewed energy enveloped the company for a while. By the mid-1980s, however, the Free was no longer the ambitious and innovative company of its early years. In 1986, the Free merged with CentreStage, where Bill Glassco was artistic director, eventually becoming the Canadian Stage Company. The Free lives on as part of what has become one of the country's largest not-for-profit contemporary theater companies, Canadian Stage.[246]

City and Grease Paint Moving into a New Era

Several other alternative theaters sprang to life in the Toronto of the 1970s and into the 1980s, including Studio Lab Theatre, Global Village Theatre, Creation 2, New Theatre, Open Circle, and the Phoenix Theatre. Many mainstream companies came online as well. A city with almost no theater companies in 1960 now had dozens.[247] Yet the creative blast of the 1970s—fed by free-spirited radicalism and nationalism—had run its course. Like Paris in the 1920s, Los Angeles in the 1930s, and London just before World War I, Toronto's 1970s energies settled into more predictable patterns.

The boom of the 1970s came to an end as quickly as it began, in large measure because of the evolution of the theater community itself. Writing in 1984, Robertson Davies, the doyen of Canadian letters, recorded that "to begin with, theatres were few and most groups interested in new plays were handicapped in their playhouses and their finances. Audiences were not warm toward Canadian plays. What they wanted from the theatre, understandably, was popular entertainment, a good night out, and they had only limited confidence that a Canadian writer and Canadian actors could provide it. There were hopeful souls, who found their way to improvised theatres to see new plays by fellow countrymen done on inadequate stages; there were a few critics who were as encouraging as they felt they could be."[248]

Other changes were afoot as well. Toronto was becoming a different city, replacing Montreal as Canada's leading urban center. Toronto's ascendance was driven by the growing economic power of its financial institutions, the arrival of tens of thousands of ambitious immigrants from around the globe, the maturation of universities and research centers, the mad rush of many non- Québécois Montrealers from that city in response to the rise of the sovereigntist Parti Québécois, and closer integration into the burgeoning continental economy led by the United States.

Toronto not only grew; it became a more expensive place to live. The warehouses that had once offered inexpensive homes to embryonic theater companies, the crash pads sheltering arriving actors, writers, and directors, as well as the once welcoming Bohemian neighborhoods such as the Annex entered into recurring cycles of gentrification that would make the city into one of the most expensive in North America. Mainstream and commercial festivals and stages—such as the O'Keeffe Center and the Royal Alexandra in Toronto, the Shaw Festival at Niagara-on-the-Lake, and the Stratford Theatre Festival—expanded their reach. Munificent government subsidies from the federal government in Ottawa and the Ontario government in Toronto, meanwhile, faced increasing budgetary scrutiny. The critics who had been so important in promoting this new theater, writers such as Herbert Whittaker and Urjo Kareda, moved on.

Audiences changed as well. An expanding urban bourgeoisie no longer sought out church pews and broken-down cinema chairs when heading out for a night on the town. They demanded more than minimal comfort as the theater and the city transformed in tandem once again during the mid-1970s. The result was a rich, varied entertainment scene where theater more than held its own. It was, like the Tarragon Theatre, not quite mainstream but no longer underground.

Toronto's remarkable growth from backwater of empire to global city created fresh opportunity for all cultural pursuits to redefine themselves and the city. Few cities were as dramatically transformed over the last half of the twentieth century. A child born into provincial Toronto in 1950, would have woken up fifty years later in one of the world's most successful and diverse cities. Toronto's theatrical explosion was both generated by and contributed to that change. The next chapter explores what happens to theater when a similarly provincial Soviet city such as Kyiv makes an even greater change to become a world capital.

Chapter 5

Kyiv in the Twenty-First Century: From Provincial City to International Capital

For the urbanist Roman Cybriwsky, postindependence Kyiv had become a "city of domes and demons."[249] Writing in 2014, just as Euromaidan demonstrators overthrew the pro-Russian national government of Viktor Yanukovych, Cybriwsky's colorful account captures the city's transformation from a provincial Soviet city to the capital of an independent country.

One profound change revolved around the city's status as a national capital. New state institutions staked their claims to prime real estate, foreign embassies opened, and districts downtown and on the Pechersk Hills near the pilgrimage site of the Pechersk Lavra (monastery) emerged as high-end districts suited for diplomats and international high rollers. The lower historic commercial area of Podil developed as hipster art districts similar to areas of New York, London, Paris, and Berlin.

Kyiv as a postsocialist city was an exemplar of another profound change. Large high-rise apartment districts dominated the suburbs, as elsewhere throughout the communist world. Single-family dwellings began to appear, scattered around the city outskirts, yet the old Soviet apartment blocks remained the city's primary housing stock.

Released from the protective bubble of the Soviet security state, Kyiv also entered the global marketplace in more negative ways. Unscrupulous and rapacious "capitalists," often former Soviet officials, divided the spoils without regard for any rules of the game, in a cityscape shaped by the survival of the fittest. A new social structure emerged crowned by a small group of the insanely wealthy, with a growing-yet-still-modest emerging professional class of bureaucrats, lawyers, accountants, and more successful entrepreneurs trying to sustain something like a middle-class lifestyle. These groups rested on a broad base of impoverished day workers, vendors, small-scale traders, and underpaid bureaucrats, petty officials, and employees of state-run educational and cultural institutions.

As Cybriwsky notes, income inequality exploded, forever altering the face of Kyiv, reaching previously unknown levels and approaching those found in middle-income countries around the world. The city's employment structure evolved, with entire new groups of shop owners, street vendors, and day laborers being added to the previous state-run Soviet scene.

Most significantly, the late Soviet city of about 2.5 million grew to somewhere over 3 million on the eve of the 2022 Russian invasion. This increase occurred despite Ukraine losing significant population, low birthrates, and high death rates. The city continued to grow in the face of constant national and local political instability. Temporary and permanent domestic migrants made up the difference, as Ukraine began to resemble other capital-dominated developing countries. A significant international migration joined the flow into the early years of this century.[250] Day laborers headed to town by the thousands, so that closer to 3.5 million people were in Kyiv on any given workday. Once a Soviet regional hub, Kyiv had become the seventh-largest city in Europe.

Long a Russian-speaking city (about 80 percent of the city's late Soviet population claimed Russian as their preferred language), Kyiv began a steady transformation to a Ukrainian-speaking one. The drive toward Ukrainian as the dominant language accelerated after the 2014 Russian annexation of Crimea and occupation of the eastern provinces of Luhansk and Donetsk. The nation's creative classes fused with ordinary Ukrainians in rejecting the language of their aggressive neighbors. They were joined by rising generations of Ukrainian youth who had become fluent in Ukrainian in school.

The city's constant political, economic, and demographic churning supported a favorable environment for the arts. Facing the challenges of developing—and, in some instances, rescuing—a distinct Ukrainian identity, a variety of arts groups and individuals sought fertile ground for expression and innovation. Visual artists, musicians, actors, writers in all genres found ready audiences among the city's expansive international community, tentative middle class, intellectuals, and young people who spent whatever disposable income they could garner on the arts. These are the Kyivians who have supported the reinvention of the city's theater scene over the past three decades.

Ukrainian Theater's Strangled Formation

Kyiv remained incorporated into the national Russian theatrical network throughout the nineteenth century until the eve of World War I. More specifically, Kyiv was a significant hub in what theater historian Mayhill C. Fowler has identified as the "Russian Imperial Southwest cultural circuit."[251] Unlike theatrical institutions in Saint Petersburg and Moscow, which were extensions of the imperial state, those in the imperial southwest were products of promoters and entrepreneurs seeking to turn a profit. Consequently, they were geared toward popular melodramas and musicals and embraced the region's notable diversity.

Kyiv and the surrounding areas on the Russian and Austria-Hungary borderlands remained a mixing bowl of peoples, cultures, and confessions. The Russian areas included much of the infamous Pale of Settlement, which remained home to Jews who were limited in their economic opportunities and ability to leave. Poles, Ukrainians, and Russians spread throughout the area, too, with Jews, Slavs, Catholic and Orthodox Christians, Hassidism, and Ashkenazi cultures coexisting alongside the Cossack heartland and Protestant (often German) enclaves. Theaters, audiences, officials, and entrepreneurs were part of the expansive network that supported all sorts of performances.

As part of the Russian Empire, cultural institutions remained subject to censorship, as did performers and writers on the Austria-Hungary side of the imperial divide. Russian censorship remained more extensive on paper than that found in Habsburg lands. The Saint Petersburg authorities, unlike their Vienna and Budapest counterparts, left censorship enforcement up to local officials. Those officials, in turn, proved to be less zealous than their imperial overseers in the capital.

Ukrainian, Polish, and Jewish promoters circumvented restrictions by working around local authorities. Jewish musicians formed the backbone of the region's musical scene and routinely received permission to leave the Pale to tour. Ukrainian entrepreneurs similarly navigated their way around the legal prohibition against Ukrainian language performances. The Tobileyvich clan's Theater of Luminaries (Teatr Koryfiev), for example, engaged in various subterfuges to play at military bases where they had been stationed. These efforts created the first Ukrainian-language theater productions, while similar circumventions nurtured Polish and Yiddish theater. As Fowler writes, "Professional Ukrainian-language theater emerged from a confluence of luck and wiliness."[252]

By the late nineteenth century, the imperial theater network had evolved into highly developed circuses, varieties, musicals, and melodramas. These unsubsidized troupes flourished as they traversed the region in search of like-minded audiences. The productions incorporated new technologies. which were transforming theatrical productions everywhere. They were less likely to reflect the artistic innovations taking place in Moscow, Saint Petersburg, and Vienna. The era of revolutions changed this picture.

A Norm of Political Upheaval

The Revolution of 1905, World War I, the Bolshevik Revolution, and the Russian Civil War shuffled the deck several times over. The Habsburg-trained theater creator Les' Kurbas ended up in Kyiv, for example, as did a number of other leaders of experimental theater who perceived the city to be safer than other locales. The result was an explosion of artistic creativity in various forms, despite the city changing hands some eighteen times as various armies came and went.[253] Prorizna Street, for example, become home to Kurbas, Stanisława Wysocka, Esther Kokhl Kaminska, Semen Semdor-Doroshenko, and Bronisława Nijinska, who all were busy inventing and reinventing Polish, Yiddish, and Ukrainian theater as well as modern dance.

The action quickly moved to Kharkiv in December 1919, after the Bolsheviks made that city the capital of their new Ukraine

Soviet Socialist Republic (the seat of Ukrainian power remained in Kharkiv until January 1934, when it moved to Kyiv). Many of the prerevolutionary artistic leaders emerging from the Russian Imperial southwest made their way to Moscow and, to a lesser extent, Leningrad, where they transformed Soviet culture.

Those controlling cultural institutions in Kharkiv were different from their counterparts in Moscow and Leningrad. Few came from an intellectual elite. Instead, Communist Party officials and Red Army officers predominated. The initial goal of creating a socialist Ukrainian-language culture trumped artistic innovation, as all the arts became increasingly dependent on the party state. A vibrant Ukrainian theater scene focused on Kharkiv flourished for a while. The 1926 Soviet census revealed that 80 percent of the republic's population declared themselves to be Ukrainian. The situation in cities, however, was different. Only 4 percent of Odesa residents identified themselves as Ukrainian. Of the 12,000 members registered with the Art Workers' Union, 40 percent were Jewish, 30 percent were Russian, and 24 percent were Ukrainian. Ukraine sponsored forty-eight theaters at the time, in eight languages (there were thirty-three Ukrainian-language theaters, seven Russian, two Yiddish, two Moldovan, one German, one Bulgarian, one Polish, and one Armenian).[254]

Kurbas's Artistic Organization Berezil' epitomized these trends.[255] Established in Kyiv in 1922, it grew to include over three hundred members working in six workshops, a directors' laboratory, a museum, and a journal. In 1926, Communist Party officials moved the group's headquarters to Kharkiv, where it could be more closely monitored. This transfer enlivened the Kharkiv theater scene, with the ever-innovative Berezil' forming a nucleus for an emerging cultural network. Yiddish- and Russian-language theaters similarly grew in Kharkiv.

Berezil' traveled around Ukraine and abroad, with particularly important performances in Berlin and Milan that helped to perfect the distinctive Ukrainian-language variety show format. These performances—such as the review *Hello from Radiowave 477!*—helped to solidify the Soviet *estrada* musical review that continues to thrive throughout Russia and its neighboring post-Soviet states. The productions similarly advanced the creation of the Ukrainian-language theatrical tradition.

However, politics soon intruded into artistic expression. The rapid industrialization and collectivization of the First Five-Year-Plan era (1928–32) required an unprecedented level of economic and political centralization. The plan's goals proved especially catastrophic in Ukraine, where centralized grain requisitions devastated the countryside, leading to the Great Famine (Holodomor) of 1930–33. The Ukrainian language and culture became a direct threat to Moscow's (and Stalin's) control. In 1934, the last remnants of the Berezil' company were transferred to the Shevchenko Theater in Kharkiv, with the top actors moving to Kyiv's Ivan Franko Theater.

Human tragedy accompanied these changes. Stalin's authoritarian meatgrinder systematically gathered up Ukraine's leading artists and intellectuals, with the "project of a modern urban Ukrainian culture," as Fowler calls it, crashing to an end. No longer able to work, Kurbas moved to Moscow in 1933, where, as he awaited his inevitable arrest, he collaborated as best he could with the Jewish actor and director Solomon Mikhoels. The knock on the door came on December 26, 1933. Kurbas joined dozens of Ukrainian cultural elites at the Belbaltlag Camp at the Solovetskii Monastary, where they were given the hard labor of building the White Sea-Baltic Canal. On November 11, 1937, Kurbas was among 134 Soviet Ukrainian artists executed that day by a firing squad.

What remained of Ukrainian theater fell under Communist Party control directed from Moscow. The destruction of Ukrainian cities during World War II and the annihilation of their Jewish populations amplified the collapse of the local theater scene, which was hardly anything other than a provincial knock-off of "All-Union" Soviet culture (despite the continuous contribution of many talented Ukrainian artists to that culture). As Fowler records, "Soviet Ukraine was increasingly not at the center of its own story."[256] This would remain so until independence in 1991.

The Czech novelist Milan Kundera, in his 1978 novel *The Book of Laughter and Forgetting*, records the dissident historian Milan Hübl as having observed in 1971 that "you begin to liquidate a people . . . by taking away its memory. You destroy its books, its culture, its history. And then others write other books for it, give another culture to it, invent another history for it. Then, the people slowly begin to forget what it is and what it was. The world at large forgets it still faster."[257]

Whether these words are those of Hübl or Kundera is immaterial. This passage perfectly captures the intent of Soviet cultural policy in Ukraine from the 1933 arrest of Ukrainian intellectuals until the collapse of the Soviet Union in 1991. After 1991, Ukrainian theater, like all Ukrainian culture, had no choice but to embark on a journey of remembering in order to move ahead. Like Kundera's and Hübl's Prague, Kyiv could only progress by recapturing its past. The city and the stage were about to embark on a shared journey.

Re-creating Ukrainian Theater

Independence brought new challenges to the Ukrainian theater scene, not the least of which was trying to continue a creative journey that had been interrupted a half century earlier. Major companies known for their Russian-language repertoire—such as Kyiv's Academic Theater of Russian Drama—found themselves politically suspect. All companies, as was the case for the other performing arts, found themselves cut loose from government funding, with few clues as to how they could survive.

The challenge for post-independence Ukrainian theater has been multifaceted. Theater-makers turned to their pre-Stalinist past to recover the creativity represented by Kurbas and those around him. They claimed artistic ownership from Moscow to create stories of their own. In doing so, they looked to Ukrainian colleagues around the country for collaboration and inspiration. Having inherited centralized budgeting and managerial practices from Soviet Ukraine, theater makers leaned on horizontal networks that were being created in response to the scarcities of independent Ukraine.

Unlike music, dance, and even opera, expatriate patrons did not pick up the slack in ticket sales, as they often resisted attending performances in a language that too many understood poorly. Furthermore, those companies holding property, such as Kyiv's Academic Theater of Russian Drama, found themselves battling ruthlessly predatory real estate developers looking to cannibalize their well-located and often prestigious properties.[258]

Theater schools, like all Ukraine's higher educational institutions, faced their own financial crises. The arts and humanities were pushed to the bottom of funding priorities, behind more practical disciplines, such as medicine, engineering, business, economics, and even political science.

Many among what might have been the founding generation for a new Ukrainian theater—such as Natal'ya Vofozhbit, Makym Kurochkin, and Sasha Denisova—made their ways to Moscow and other Russian theater centers, attracted by more robust audiences and financial support. Russian theater in the late 1990s and into the early 2000s surged with what became known as the "New Russian Drama" movement, which elevated unsparingly tough, often profane, looks at that society's numerous ills. That drama, in turn, reinvigorated Russian television, which similarly offered bountiful opportunities absent in Ukraine.

This reinvigorated Russian theatrical scene commanded international attention and funding beyond anything evident in Ukraine at the time. Russian theater's creative outburst, however, ran its course by the 2010s, as it came under heightened attack from the Russian Orthodox Church's morality monitors, which were aligned with the reemerging authoritarian security state.[259]

The bleak picture in Ukraine began to brighten at the outset of the twenty-first century. A generation coming of age during independence discovered theater as a means for exploring their own lives. Small, experimental companies emerged in numerous provincial cities. Shoe-string productions popped up in and around regional universities, where they attracted student playwrights, directors, actors, and audiences.

In 2003, for example, Ruslana and Pavlo Porytski, two students at Volyn State University in the western Ukrainian city of Lutsk, created the experimental GaRmYdEr (Garmyder) theater in an unremarkable metal hanger—what Americans call a "Quonset hut." The hanger stands in rail yards once used by both the Nazis and Soviets to dispatch prisoners to concentration camps.[260]

Taking its name from an expression roughly translated as "a little of this, and a little of that," the company reached out to the neighboring community for support. Surrounded by textile and candy factories, the building became a gathering place for theatergoers, children attending their first performances, rock bands, and international touring groups. Among their most noteworthy productions, the *Princely Banquet* in 2017 brought together visiting choruses from Lviv and an equestrian theater troupe to celebrate Prince Vytautas, his retinue, knights, traditional dance, and songs. Later, they honored the late poet Kost Shyshko, who was executed by the Soviet regime, by staging readings of his works at an unfinished high-rise building. On each floor, including the roof, there were immersive events based on his poems and his life.

Starting out on small chamber stages at the university, and moving to the local House of Culture, the Porytskis attracted enthusiastic collaborators. By 2022, the troupe had grown into a self-managing company of some fifty actors, directors, editors, camera operators, administrators, and writers. Their story was being repeated all over Ukraine, as the new Ukrainian-language theater came into being.

Pavlo Bosy, the producer at the Little Globe Theater in Kirovohrad, a provincial center southeast of Kyiv, argued that theater had become "that kind of art, which is the most alive, metaphoric, and capable of reacting to life issues."[261] Consequently, it is a singular art form for wrestling with notions of a model society. By the turn of the twenty-first century, Bosy observed, Ukrainian theater in the regions had become "a baroque carnival," with directors and playwrights starting to reach back to draw upon images and themes from history in order to reinterpret them.

Some of this new work found its way to Kyiv by the early 2000s, where it joined with the capital's increasingly vigorous theater scene to create the new Ukrainian theater. The establishment of the Les' Kurbas State Centre for Theatre Arts in December 1994 offered an important hub for this new scene. Charged with bringing together new influences from abroad with trends within Ukrainian theater, the center opened in 1996. The program's mix of scholarly research and theater practice generated new ideas, nurtured young talent, and integrated Ukrainian theater into the broader global theater world.[262]

These developments, both within the capital and around the country, stimulated middle-class audiences with disposable incomes and, perhaps more important, their children, to discover theater's power to confront society's most troublesome issues. European cultural foundations, such as the British Council and the Goethe Institute, generously invested in theater as part of their initiatives to foster a democratic Ukraine.

From Soviet to Ukrainian

Simultaneously, Soviet-era institutions—such as the Lesya Ukrainka and Ivan Franko theaters—reinvented themselves. Among Kyiv's oldest and most important performance groups, the Lesya Ukrainka Theater traces its roots back to the Solovtsov acting troupe, which began in 1891, before evolving into the Kyiv Russian Drama Theater. After World War II, the company was named in honor of the national poet Lesya Ukrainka (the penname of Larysa Petrivna Kosach). The theater retained this title until the 2022 full-scale Russian invasion, when the theater dropped "Russian Drama" from its name.

The company has performed in the historic Bourgogne Theater for nearly a century. Opened by the French mogul Auguste Bergonier in 1875, the building hosted the city circus and then an early cinema before being given over to what became the Lesya Ukrainka company in 1929. Located at the very center of the city, the theater and company have long been honored; and they have hosted some of imperial Russia's, the Soviet Union's, and Ukraine's most illustrious theater artists.

Favored by Soviet cultural and Communist Party officials, the company entered a troubled transition after 1991, as independence severed connections to Moscow's financial support and its overt embrace of "Russian" theater became a liability. Under the direction of Mykhailo Yuriiovych Reznikovych since 1994, the company has worked to sustain its rich historic repertoire as it has repositioned itself within an increasingly Ukrainian-language involvement. Its "Under the Roof" series, performed in the theater's attic, focuses on contemporary and avant-garde productions. The symbolic dropping of "Russian" from its name in 2022 acknowledged the company's long-term trajectory toward a more fulsome embrace of its Ukrainian roots.[263]

The city's Ivan Franko National Academic Drama Theater similarly served as a cornerstone for Kyiv's late-twentieth-century theater scene. Known for promoting works that have played an important role in Ukrainian cultural history, the company traces its roots back to 1920. Founded in Vinnytsia, with actors from Lviv, after that city's transfer to newly independent Poland, the company moved around Soviet Ukraine before settling in Kharkiv, and then in Kyiv. Once in Kyiv, the company settled into the building that had opened in 1898 to house the Solovtsov Theater, one of the most beautiful arts venues in Ukraine. The company increasingly partnered with Les Kurbas's Berezil' during these years. As noted above, when the Ukrainian authorities disbanded Berezil' in 1934, many of that company's actors transferred to the Ivan Franko.

The company suffered from the imposition of a propagandistic repertoire during the 1930s and, after wartime evacuation to Semipalatinsk and Tashkent, into the 1960s. Its productions and its reputation began to change during the 1970s as the company, headed by Serhiy Danchenko between 1978 and 2001, became known for its stunning scenography and musical programs. The theater gained a reputation for its productions of classics by Ibsen, Shakespeare, and Chekov that highlight the moral quandaries of the late Soviet period. Like the Lesya Ukrainka theater, the Ivan Franko company struggled with the financial uncertainties of the early postindependence years. By the twenty-first century, it was once again earning kudos for its innovative works, including its Chamber Scene small stage productions, which began in 2012.[264]

Other established companies, such as the National Academic Operetta Theater, similarly sought to reposition themselves. Another landmark theater from an era when theaters were viewed as confections, the theater endured calamities and tragedies despite its grand appearance. Constructed with charitable contributions at the turn of the twentieth century as the Trinity People's House, the building initially housed the Kyiv Society of Literacy and other artistic organizations. It became home to several educational, sports, political, and labor organizations after the Bolshevik Revolution, before being turned over as a home for musical theater in 1934. After independence, the company turned to the West, entering into collaborative arrangements with Liverpool's Eurovision Cultural

Program, Vienna's Musiktheatrtage, and Frankfurt's Theater der Welt.[265]

In 2000, theater students from the Kyiv National University of Theatre, Film, and Television established the Theater on Pechersk under the direction of their professor at the time, Nikolay Rushkovsky, and the longtime theater director Alexander Kryzhanovsky. Over the past quarter century, this company has developed a distinctive repertoire and style that represent fresh directions in Ukrainian theater. Its combinations of new works (e.g., *Under Pressure / Push-Up1-2-3*) and new takes on long-standing plays (e.g., its innovative production of *Man of La Mancha*) have won awards in Ukraine and around Europe. The company has served as a vital launching pad for the careers of actors, directors, and producers, who now fill Ukrainian stages and screens.[266]

These institutional and artistic developments—which were accompanied by the appearance of numerous smaller companies—transpired against the backdrop of political turmoil. The upheavals of the Orange Revolution (2004–5) and the Euromaidan and Revolution of Dignity (2013–14) provided generous fodder for new works.

Both events focused on Kyiv's central Maidan Nezalezhnosti, Independence Square. The Maidan was the perfect location for such public demonstrations. Nestled in a small valley among various fragments of the overall city (Pechersk, "Old Kyiv," Berssarabka, Podil', etc.), the Maidan exerts a central gravitational force, giving form and definition to Kyiv's urban life. As many as a dozen streets flow down into the Maidan; and the city's primary avenue, the Khreshchatyk, runs through it. Nearly all the city's major institutions, including the theaters mentioned here, are located nearby. Apartment houses built for prominent members of the Soviet regime similarly sit within walking distance; many occupied with residents ready to cook a warm meal to feed demonstrators camped on their doorsteps. Connected to the entire city by several subway and major bus lines, the Maidan was a natural space for civic life before demonstrators turned it orange. Protesters head straight for this space whenever political turbulence bubbles over into the streets.

This morphology made the politics of Ukrainian independence and nationhood an intensely urban affair. Kyiv increasingly gathered up Ukraine's theater talent, despite noteworthy theatrical scenes in Kharkiv, Lviv, Dnipro, Odesa, and elsewhere. Once in Kyiv, these artists looked to the city for inspiration. Kyiv itself was becoming an agent of its own artistic dynamism.

Ukrainian theater and other arts evolved in tandem with changes in the nation and its political life, and the city and its urban development. Several of these trends coalesced after the Russian seizure of Crimea and portions of Donetsk and Luhansk in 2014 to form a new theatrical enterprise in Kyiv.

2014: A War Begins

Over the past three decades, young Ukrainians have created a lively and distinctive popular culture through music—including their own brand of hip-hop—and social media. Ukrainian youth culture has triumphed over internal differences across the country. Ukrainian has been the language of this culture. Whether cultivated by official and commercial outlets—for example, *The Simpsons* appeared in Ukrainian rather than Russian translation—or homegrown social media formats—this new culture has remained, first and foremost, fun.

More established cultural forms—literature and theater among them—have lagged behind this trend. Major Ukrainian writers continued to write in Russian well into the 2000s. Russian had been the language they spoke at home growing up, and the Russian reading public extended far beyond that of Ukraine. Moreover, many potential Ukrainian readers could plough effortlessly through their works in Russian.

Similarly, in the theater some playwrights, directors, and actors worked in Russia as the larger scene there created more opportunities to expand their horizons. A Kyiv native, Maksym Kurochkin, for example, became one of the New Russian Drama movement's brightest stars. He worked in Moscow, in the post-Soviet theatrical hotbed of Yekaterinburg, and in the Russian film industry. The playwright Natalka Vorozhbut graduated from the Maxim Gorky

Literature Institute in Moscow and moved seamlessly into the worlds of Russian theater, cinema, and television. The playwright Neda Nejdana's remarkable plays appeared on stages in Ukraine, Russia, Britain, and North America. Sasha Denisova participated in creating the documentary theater movement focused on Moscow's fearless Teatr.doc, which was founded in 2002 by the playwrights Elena Gremina and Mikhail Ugarov and was shut down after their deaths in 2018. Denisova also served as deputy director of Moscow's Mayakovsky Theater and won Russia's prestigious Golden Mask Award in 2021 for her play *Light My Fire*.

Kurochkin and nineteen other playwrights came together in 2020 to form the Theater of Playwrights, which intended to join forces to create a theater whose main value would be the text at the center of their work. The group began presenting their own works, creating opportunities for other writers to exchange their plays, and offered training to young playwrights. This began at a time when the organizers estimated that fewer than 15 percent of works on Ukrainian stages were of Ukrainian origin. These works increasingly were in the Ukrainian language (Kurochkin himself switch to writing in Ukrainian). The group drew on its international ties to raise foreign funds to support its effort. This and other initiatives intended to nurture the new Ukrainian theater stalled during the COVID-19 pandemic but began to regain energy as 2021 came to a close.[267]

Another major project reflects the desire of Kyiv's theater community to respond to the growing challenge to Ukraine's sovereignty in the east. Despite COVID restrictions, the director Dmytro Kostiumynskyi and his team with the DollMen Theater Company managed to bring its *Ukrainian Odyssey* project together in 2020.[268] Inspired by the ongoing war in Eastern Ukraine, their project considered war, revolution, and heroism through five episodes set in postapocalyptic cities performed through dramatic and physical theater, virtual reality, and puppetry.

Kostiumynskyi formed DollMen in 2014 and established connections with like-minded European theater directors. His production that year, *Hamlet: Babylon*, combined contemporary music, video scenography, and interactive modern media to show Shakespeare's Danish prince constructing and destroying a personal world in an unstable virtual environment. This work played in Geneva, where it won encouraging reviews.

Kostiumynskyi and the company turned to Ukrainian matters with the stunning 2021 production *Crimea, 5 am*, dedicated to political prisoners, telling the story of human rights violations in Russian-occupied Crimea. Kostyiumynskyi feared that the human tragedies of the prisoners—who often are seized in their homes at 5 am—and their families were becoming abstractions. He asked the playwrights Natalka Vorozhbyt and Anastasia Kosodiy to write scripts based on interviews with activists to create a documentary text. The production and accompanying videos and books brought the human dimension of incarceration back to the center of Ukrainian attention.

Kostiumynskyi teamed up with the performing artist, choreographer-researcher, dancer, producer, curator, and educator Viktor Ruban to launch the *Ukrainian Odyssey*. Together they planned a five-city tour (Kyiv–Lviv–Kharkiv–Odesa–Kyiv), offering a contemporary take on Homer's *Odyssey* and James Joyce's *Ulysses*. They hoped to encourage audiences to travel throughout the country and to see segments performed by different artists in other cities.

Their parade of performances across Ukraine's major cities had made only three stops when it landed at Kharkiv's NEFT puppet theater just weeks before Russia launched its full-scale invasion in February 2022. What had been virtual and theoretical before now became immediate and tangible. *Ukrainian Odyssey* hit the pause button, as most of the company members headed off to war and recreational travel around Ukraine came to a halt.

Its creators continued to redefine the project in light of the continuing war. In mid-2022, with Kostiumynskyi off at the front lines, the Lviv Academic Dramatic Lesia Theater staged a re-premier, adding accents prompted by the new war.

The Ukrainian Odyssey project illustrates how the Russian incursion into Crimea in 2014 changed the theater world in the Kyiv and throughout Ukraine. Youth culture, even among Russian-language rappers in Eastern Ukraine, switched solely to using the Ukrainian language. Writers of both prose and poetry began writing in Ukrainian, even when it was not their first language. Theater artists found that Ukrainian better communicated their emotions and world view in light of a Russian aggression that only made them feel more Ukrainian. In theater, as in dance and music, leading writers and directors began to return home.

The war also forced many in Eastern Ukraine's theater community to head west, settling in Kyiv, Lviv, and elsewhere. Many of these displaced artists would make important contributions to Ukrainian theater in the years ahead.

The Theater at War

"When you hear the sound of a shell flying at your house, at first you feel fear, then hatred. Hatred for whoever did it. For all of Russia, for all inhabitants without exception." This line, from the first-person narrator in Olena Astaseva's play *A Dictionary of Emotions in a Time of War*, reveals profound truths about the future of Ukrainian–Russian relations after Russia's full-scale invasion launched on February 24, 2022.

This observation comes from one of the many dozens of plays commissioned by Kurochkin, working in collaboration with the theater writer John Freedman, Philip Arnoult of Baltimore's Center for International Theater Development, and Noah Birksted-Breen of London's Sputnik Theatre through the Worldwide Ukrainian Play Readings Project. Launched just days after the 2022 invasion, the project commissioned playwrights to write new works based on their wartime experiences. The plays—which number in the hundreds—have been translated into English and other languages and offered at scores of readings before audiences in dozens of countries. Some eventually went into full production. Cumulatively, these efforts have raised tens of thousands of dollars for direct aid, medical supplies, and food for Ukrainian hospitals, shelters, food distribution centers, and elder care facilities.

The project's success rested on the networks of playwrights and theater artists nurtured by Kurochkin and others in the years leading up to 2022. Kurochkin and his colleagues not only took Ukrainian theater abroad; they also brought it to Kyiv with a triumphant marathon session at the Theater of Playwright's unfinished basement in June 2022.[269]

These works demonstrate how theater's artificiality opens up opportunities for truth-telling uninhibited by ordinary life's injunctions. The plays collectively respond to the experience of Ukrainians on the ground, trying to answer unanswerable questions. Their primal sentiments are expressed on stage, where profound truths of human existence can be voiced openly.

Kurochkin and his collaborators brought exciting Ukrainian theater to an international community unfamiliar with Kyiv's vibrant scene. In October 2022, for example, Blank Space Studio HK joined with the Worldwide Ukrainian Play Readings campaign to stage a dozen new plays in Hong Kong. Produced and directed by Donald Chung, Amy Sze, and William Wong, the festival presented six productions from seven directors with twenty-eight actors on two consecutive weekends. Chung, Sze, and Wong were unfamiliar with Ukrainian theater before the Russian invasion. Sze was studying for a master's degree in London. She met a classmate from Moscow with a Ukrainian cultural background and was drawn to the play readings organized by the Worldwide Ukrainian Play Readings Project.[270]

Chung was also in London. As a theater maker, he set out to find Ukrainian plays in bookstores, only to be disappointed by how little Londoners and other Europeans knew about their neighbors. Recalling similar disinterest in Hong Kong about events in Thailand, Myanmar, and elsewhere in Asia, Chung began to think about how to use theater to break down walls of unfamiliarity. He too sought out the Worldwide Ukrainian Play Reading project's London readings.

The Hong Kong theater's leading light, William Wong, made his own discovery of Ukrainian plays during the weeks after the Russian invasion. While he had never thought of Ukrainian plays before, the opportunity to read Natalya Vorozhbit's *Bad Roads* led him to think about what was happening. His Blank Space Studio brought a reading of *Bad Roads* to the local stage shortly after the outbreak of the war.

Their effort to stage Ukrainian works helped Hong Kong's audiences understand what was happening in Ukraine in a more direct way than the sporadic stories appearing in the local media. The works spoke to their own ordeals in perhaps unexpected ways. The three festival organizers found the Ukrainian works address general human themes about war, suffering, the wrenching experience of civilians in conflict, and how to mobilize feeling like a victim to positive ends.

The Worldwide Readings Project has had a double effect. First, it has sustained theatrical creativity and networks within war-torn Ukraine, opening possibilities for a dynamic theater scene in Kyiv and elsewhere once the war has ended. Second, it has made the international community aware of the consolidation of a vibrant theater community within Ukraine. Consequently, in recent years, Ukrainian plays have regularly appeared on stages from London to Hong Kong, from New York to Buenos Aires.

Despite signs of resilience, the Russian invasion of Ukraine has, in the words of the well-known Ukrainian theater critic and scholar Hanna Veselovska, victimized the Ukrainian theater "doubly and perhaps even triply through the ongoing hostilities. The Ukrainian theatre has been losing its space, because its home, an artistic setting, is crumbling; it has been losing its creative potential, because its artists are being killed or scattered around the world; it has been deprived of the opportunity to communicate with the viewer, that is, to create art, which is a central means of preserving human civilization."[271] All these efforts are part of a concerted Russian effort to destroy Ukrainian culture.

Simultaneously, she continues, Ukrainian theater has taken decisive steps since the Russian invasion to speak more actively in the voice of hypermodern drama. Turning their back on Russian theater, Ukrainian theater artists are resorting to symbolization through movement, colors, silhouettes, light, individual rhythmic scenes, and the stylistics of archaic and folklore rituals, which open the door to a vibrant postwar era. "The tragedy of the war," she notes, "has also been an impetus for the Ukrainian theatre to move beyond local settings and connect with the international community." Freed from the strangling grip of Russia, Ukrainian theater, to return to Fowler, finally stands at the center of its own story.[272]

Theater as Ukraine's Safe Space

As theaters reopened under martial law strictures, their staging of new and old works provided both relief from the hardships of war and opportunities to nurture public dialogue about its displacements. Ukraine's collective and personal responses to war's traumas have been dramatically visible from its stages.

Iulia Bentia and Pavlo Shopin, two Ukrainian theater scholars, undertook a foray into what wartime theater reveals about their society's traumas, aspirations, and dispositions in an article in the journal *Art History in Ukraine* (*Mystetstvoznavstvo*).[273] They turned to submissions made for the fifth All-Ukrainian Festival organized in 2023 by the National Union of Theater Artists of Ukraine. Dating from 2017, the festival has presented productions by companies large and small, from every corner of the country. No festival took place in 2022, so the 2023 festival presented 134 performances ranging from plays for children to large-scale productions, from musicals to experimental works.

Eighteen of the plays related directly to the current war. These contemporary wartime works explored the challenges of emigration, tests of mental health, and a range of moral issues surrounding key questions of loyalty, violence, and the meaning of community.

Bentia and Shopin were particularly interested in how recent traumas of war have reshaped interpretations of classical theatrical works, and how those works empower audiences to think differently about their own daily trials. They examined four productions in particular: Ivan Franko Theater's stagings of Albert Camus's *Caligula* and Lesya Ukrainka's dramatic poem *Cassandra*; Theater on Podil's production of Sophocles's *Oedipus Rex*; and Poltava Puppet Theater's *The Great Dungeon*, based on Taras Shevchenko's "mystery poem." These productions reimagined classic theatrical works while considering current events, both shedding new insight into the works themselves and framing painful conversations about the dislocations of the current war.

The authors argued that theater provides a safe social space for public discussion seeking to understand the traumas imposed by the current war. *Caligula* raised penetrating insights into the brutality and immorality of authoritarian rule and contributed to media discussions about the mental health of the Russian president. *Oedipus* related to the growing demand for justice in wartime society at a time when discussions over morality are gaining in importance. *Cassandra* explored the ways in which humans protect themselves by constructing fanciful illusions. Shevchenko's work sets the current conflict against the backdrop of previous Russo-Ukrainian wars.

Bentia and Shopin concluded that each of the festival's productions—both those only two months old and those written two millennia ago—provided a safe space for emotional responses to shared tragedy. While acknowledging that the full-scale Russian invasion has attracted unprecedented attention to Ukrainian theater both at home and abroad, they are most interested in the social aspects of theater that help uncover how Ukrainians understand and overcome the traumatic experiences of war.

A Fringe That Became a Center

At first glance, the opening night of the 2023 Kyiv Fringe Festival might have been taking place at any contemporary theater in the world. Theater people—some with bright orange hair, some with neon blue hair; sporting T shirts (often black) and baseball caps, well-loved Panama hats, and at least one Donegal flat cap; clad in shorts and jeans—gathered around a long table overflowing with wine, grapes, and cheese set out under florescent lights to celebrate the synergy of live performance. Only the organizer's promise of a Ukrainian victory that would empower an even brighter future for other such festivals signaled that there was nothing commonplace about this year's jubilee edition.[274]

The festival, the fifth such program since its inception in 2018, has continued to connect the Ukrainian theater scene with the broader international theatrical community, despite the pandemic and war. Organized by the National Les Kurbas Centre, the festival grew out of an initial proposal from Alex Borovenskiy, the artistic director of ProEnglish Theatre of Ukraine, and Steve Gove, founder of Prague Fringe. Their goal, from the beginning, has been to increase awareness of international creative movements in Ukraine, and to expand knowledge about the Ukrainian theater scene abroad. The festival has gained greater meaning since the 2022 Russian invasion, which has sought to isolate Ukraine and Ukrainian culture.

The 2023 festival—which ran between August 31 and September 3—included a dozen English-language performances featuring participants from Britain, the United States, France, Switzerland, Hong Kong, and Ukraine. Performers rendered a variety of theatrical genres, from Butoh to stand-up comedy, and from experimental works to a traditional detective story. Workshops and master classes filled out the schedule, as did multiple opportunities for Ukrainian actors to showcase their talents in front of audiences and jurors. Stand Up Open Mic evenings performed in English augmented these events. Parallel online performances from Britain featured nearly two dozen additional works from England, Ireland, Italy, and Canada.

Organizers described that year's edition as a "festival for the brave," featuring works already performed abroad, such as Neda Nejdana's *Pussycat in Memory of Darkness*, and those unknown outside the country, such as Borovenskiy's *Naïve Experiment*, based on the Norwegian novelist Erlend Loe's bestseller *Naïve: Super*.

The Kyiv live performances exposed tensions between good and evil and cast a fresh light on the challenges of living through an intense trauma. For example, *Naïve Experiment* tells the story of a twenty-something man who suddenly becomes confused by life. He leaves his parents, drops out of a university, and moves in with his brother. He regains a sense of life by throwing a ball against the wall, riding a bicycle, and making lists. *Be My Marguerite! (Or in the Strangeness of Loneliness)*, performed by the Swiss actor Madeleine Bongard, follows the inner world of M, a character based on interviews given by the French author Marguerite Duras. This play explores the connections between our bodies and our inner worlds.

Tomas K. H. Tse, from Hong Kong's Theatre Aether, drew on the Butoh tradition to tell the story of Lu-Ting, whose name is forbidden to be spoken, in *To-To: A Fairy Tale of Lu-Ting*. The festival closed with Daniel Gerroll's performance in *Dr. Glas*, crafted by the playwright Jeffrey Hatcher into a solo piece based on the Swedish author Hjalmar Söderberg's 1905 novel about a Stockholm doctor grappling with romantic and moral issues.

These and other festival works highlight the importance of courage and resilience in the face of human calamity and tragedy. Audience members and actors—both from down the block and from as far away as Hong Kong and the United States—carried on despite air raid sirens and lethal rocket attacks. If previous Kyiv fringe festivals revealed a world of alternative theater beyond Ukraine to local audiences, the 2023 gathering showcased Ukrainian creativity to the international participants.

In reflecting on the 2023 festival, the organizer Borovenskiy observed: "As for the first time, Ukraine Fringe gathered a tremendous response. Within four days in Kyiv, we had nineteen performances from eight artistic teams from different countries. The audience attended each and every show. It feels that Ukraine needs Ukraine Fringe especially these days. This festival represents Ukraine of the future, Ukraine that wins the war, Ukraine that is open to Europe and the whole world. Ukraine that is free. Next year we are definitely going to continue with Ukraine Fringe. We'd love to conduct it in liberated Mariupol or Crimea."

A few days before the festival's opening, on Ukraine's Independence Day, August 24, the organizers posted a statement on Facebook: "We stand with each and every Ukrainian shoulder to shoulder in our desire to keep and nourish our independent country. The Ukraine Fringe Festival was specifically meant to be built around Ukraine's Independence Day. This is exactly how we see our country: free, diverse, strong, funny, and international."

Those who attended and performed at the 2023 wartime festival, both in person and online, understand that Kyiv's theater has a future. This festival suggests that Kyiv's theater community will be able to stare down any brutal enemy. It demonstrates how, after more than a century of effort, the Ukrainian theatrical community that has taken root in Kyiv both honors their country's and their city's past and engages the outside theatrical world with confidence.

The stories from Montreal, Washington, Toronto, and Kyiv illustrate how urban growth creates wealth and nurtures the audiences necessary to support the arts. In each instance, the arts, in turn, help communities work through the divisions of language, race, generational change, and postcolonialism. The story of Nashville reverses the causal arrows. The next chapter reveals how success in the performing arts—especially of a commercialized performing art form, such as country music—can elevate a city to previously unimagined heights. Each story illustrates the complex relationships between stages which must shift in response to cities that are changing around them.

Chapter 6

Nashville: Music Makes the Town: The Growth of Country Music and the City's Rise

The musical genre known today as "Country Music" is, to a considerable extent, a commercial creation–not the music itself, but how it has been collected, produced, and marketed. Record producers a century ago, looking for new ways to grow the audience for their products, hunted rural America for musicians to promote. Beyond classical, popular, and stage music, the new companies captured jazz, creating a list of "Race Music" to be promoted to African Americans. Some producers, looking to an expanding market in South America, recorded Tango and other popular musical forms. Still others traveled up and down the byways of the Appalachians, Texas, and elsewhere looking for performers who could bring "Hillbilly" music to life. Centered in New York, the industry's recruiting efforts initially remained dispersed geographically. But over time, the recording studios became centralized, as recording production commodified and connected with rising radio broadcasting outlets. Nashville would emerge in time as a central node in this process. The music industry, in turn, triggered Nashville's rise as a global city.

Scouring the Countryside for Talent

Thirty-one-year-old recording entrepreneur Ralph Peer left his hometown of Independence, Missouri, shortly after the end of World War I in search of new music to record for the General Phonograph Corporation's OKeh Label. The plan was to track down folk music in the languages of various immigrant groups to sell to their communities.

Founder Otto K. E. Heinemann (hence "OKeh") started selling records in 1916 and moved to making them in 1918 at a New York pressing plant. Peer, one of Heinemann's scouts, "discovered" Blues singer Mamie Smith, who recorded "Crazy Blues" for the label in 1920. Black Pullman porters began buying and reselling the recording on their runs around the country, leading OKeh to launch a list of "Race Records," which brought many of jazz's pioneers—including King Oliver, Louis Armstrong, and Bix Beiderbecke—to wider audiences. The growing Columbia Records Company bought the OKeh label in 1926.[275]

Sensing new rural markets for OKeh recordings, Peer wanted to start a white list of "Hillbilly" music to parallel the company's successful line of "Race Records" featuring Black artists. By 1923, he had set up shop in Atlanta and started recording both Black and white artists, including the emerging star Fiddlin' John Carson.[276] Meanwhile, his competitor, the Victor Talking Machine Company, had signed the Texas fiddler Eck Robertson. The commercial music genre first known as "Hillbilly" music—and, later, as "Country and Western," and, presently, more simply as "Country"—was launched.

The music, of course, predated this birth by decades, even centuries. European immigrants brought their musical memories and their instruments (e.g., fiddles, guitars, and mandolins) with them to the so-called New World. African slaves brought their musical memories and, as soon as possible, recreated their drums and a West African stringed instrument, the *bandore*, which evolved on this side of the Atlantic into the banjo. Scottish migrants settling in Appalachia played sea chanties, hymns, and ballads of longing and sorrow; or upbeat music for community "square dances." Slaves developed the Blues from their earlier traditions, and a local religious musical tradition that would evolve into Gospel Music during the twentieth century.

Musical entrepreneurs commercialized this music as early as the 1840s. A Cincinnati bookkeeper named Stephen Foster began writing songs for monetary profit. His tunes—such as "Oh! Susanna," "Camptown Races," "Old Folks at Home," "My Old Kentucky Home," and "Old Black Joe"—became part of the American musical canon and continue to be sung and enjoyed more than a century and a half later.[277] They proved to be well suited for the "blackface minstrel" variety shows that dominated American popular culture, both in its original and in its evolved form, as so-called vaudeville variety theater. At the outset of the 1850s, Foster entered into a contract to write songs for the Christy Minstrels.

Edwin Pearce Christy had moved in 1825, at the age of ten, from his native Pennsylvania to New Orleans, arriving in that Caribbean-tinged city reflecting its French, Spanish, and African origins.[278] The young northern boy was drawn to the famous African drumming circles that gathered every Sunday afternoon on Congo Square. After joining the touring Purdy, Welch & Delavan Menagerie and Circus in 1832, Christy returned to New Orleans and found a job supervising slaves at a local rope works. In 1846, he set out for Buffalo, where he formed Christy's Minstrels, who quickly moved to New York to start a ten-year run as one of the most popular shows in town. This native-born genre flowed into the mix that would become Country Music.

Peer and Heinemann, thus, pursued a long-standing American practice of turning music into a profitable enterprise. Peer joined other recording scouts in searching for undiscovered white rural talents, whom he sent off to New York studios to record.[279] The automobile entrepreneur Henry Ford supported some of these efforts—appalled, as he was, by the rise of jazz, which he considered to be a Black and Jewish plot to weaken the white race. There was money to be made from the "Hillbilly" sound.

The more Peer and his colleagues searched, the more talent they found. Some came from musical hotspots such as Bristol on the Virginia and Tennessee border; others from the Texas lowland; and still others from the deep gorges of Appalachia—including musicians such as A. P. Carter and his family members Maybelle and Sara, Dr. Dr. Humphrey Bates and the Possum Hunters, Jimmy Rodgers, Uncle Dave Macon, and the Black harmonica wizard DeFord Bailey. These and other musicians traveled across the South, building the foundation for a single genre that arose from multiple musical styles.

Record company executives turned to another new technology that simultaneously created an entire new industry: radio.[280] Radio spread quickly after the federal government granted the first broadcast license to Pittsburgh's KDKA in 1920. Station managers needed to fill airtime, and record companies needed to spread the word about their latest recordings. The twentieth-century American commercial music industry was born.

Many of the early radio stations extended from previously existing retailers looking to push their merchandise. Stations such as Kansas City's KFKB ("Kansas First, Kansas Best"); Iowa's KFNF ("Keep Friendly, Never Frown"); Fort Worth's WBAP, which pioneered square dance programs; and the biggest of all, Sears, Roebuck & Company's Chicago flagship station, WLS ("World's Largest Store").[281]

With a reach throughout the Midwest, WLS pioneered several program formats featuring dance bands, classical music, plays, sports, and religious services. On April 19, 1926, WLS launched a new program featuring "Hillbilly" music, the *National Barn Dance*. At some point, as noted above, WLS's radio waves reached Nashville, where Edwin Craig, the son of a local insurance scion, had the idea of selling coverage on the airwaves. Launching the radio station WSM ("We Shield Millions") in 1925 from the insurance company's downtown Nashville headquarters, Craig established a new program format: *WSM Barn Dance*. By 1927, the show would be renamed *The Grand Ole Opry*.[282] Nashville had entered the race to become one of the new centers of this ever-more-popular (and lucrative) music industry.

Taking to the Airways

Throughout the last century, Nashville's rise to become America's "Music City" has wound through *The Grand Ole Opry* many times over. What began as a local operation selling insurance policies expanded into a regional powerhouse when WSM secured one of only three federal licenses in the South at the time to broadcast as a 50,000 watt "clear channel" station.[283]

The Opry won fans throughout the South and beyond (listeners could tune in across thirty states, primarily on the East Coast). A few years later, the station extended the program's reach by joining the national NBC Red Network (one of a handful of national broadcasting syndicates, including the American Broadcasting System, the Columbia Broadcasting System, and the Mutual Broadcasting System).

With WSM's studios no longer able to accommodate an expanding audience, the station moved to ever larger venues such as the Hillsboro Theatre, the Dixie Tabernacle, and the War Memorial Auditorium. In June 1943, WSM set up shop in the Ryman Auditorium (the former Union Gospel Tabernacle) dating from 1892, which had begun hosting nonreligious shows, lectures, and sporting events during the early twentieth century to pay off debts. *The Opry* remained at the Ryman until 1974, when the country show moved to the specially built Opryland entertainment complex east of town.[284]

Edwin Craig perhaps had more modest goals at the outset. He and the other WSM managers concluded that sending recordings and live acts out over the airwaves was insufficient to meet the demand. They began arranging for regional tours after *The Opry*'s weekly broadcast ended and returning in time to perform live once more before the Nashville audience. The tours demanded teams of performers—both frontmen and studio musicians—technicians, composers, promoters, even bus drivers.

Nashville became a magnet for the sorts of folks who were needed to keep the music playing. They moved out into the community, performing and working around town whenever they were freed from their obligations at WSM. Craig's station thus became an animating force generating the creative, social, and technological infrastructure that would turn Nashville from just another indistinguishable state capital into a musical juggernaut. None of this happened at once.

WSM faced increasing competition because managers of other radio stations knew a good thing when they saw it. Regional stations adapted similar barn-dance formats in as dispersed locales as Tulsa, Oklahoma (KVOO); Charlotte, North Carolina (WBT's *Crazy Barn Dance*); and Wheeling, West Virginia (WWVA's *Jamboree*). Chicago's WLS continued to dominate the scene, attracting audiences in the thousands to its *National Barn Dance* well into the 1930s.²⁸⁵ New musicians and styles continued to emerge across rural America, from the Alabama and Mississippi flatlands to Appalachia's Mountain counties, out through Texas and, increasingly, in California. An increasingly media-savvy generation of musicians—such as Gene Autry, Patsy Montana, Tex Ritter, and Bob Willis—took the music to Broadway and Hollywood.²⁸⁶

Craig and the WSM team, however, had their own magic touch (assisted, no doubt, by their willingness to pay performers top dollar). As the songwriter-turned-music-historian Michael Kosser notes, "*The Opry* was different from the other radio shows." Craig and the WSM team, he continues, "went on a massive talent drive to attract all of the hot hunks of the day."²⁸⁷ *The Opry*'s Saturday night time slot, combined with the station's 50,000 watt platform, ensured a devoted listenership.²⁸⁸ *The Opry*'s reach expanded further in 1939, when the RJ Reynolds Tobacco Company sponsored its move to the NBC Radio Network, giving the program a nationwide reach.

Young listeners, some of whom would themselves become *Opry* stars in the future, discovered the music on their home radios, and they formed a self-perpetuating fan base that carried the show for decades. This success rested primarily on its talented lineup, which featured the Carter Family (followed by the Carter Sisters), Roy Acuff, Bill Monroe, and the beloved comedienne Minnie Pearl (Sara Ophelia Colley). *The Opry*'s regulars became beloved family members, as Depression-era audiences across rural America gathered every Saturday to listen. This success enabled WSM to attract newcomers looking for their first break. The accompanying road trips cemented the bond between performers and audiences as detached voices from the family radio turned into three-dimensional human beings.

The Opry's broadcasts emanated from a live weekly performance, which steadily grew to attract hundreds of audience members, many from great distances across the South. As noted above, the show moved to the Hillsboro Theater, and then to the Dixie Tabernacle. In some ways, East Nashville's Dixie Tabernacle—a large barn with sawdust floors and bench seating accommodating about one thousand listeners—captured *The Opry*'s atmosphere and personality. The show nonetheless moved to the larger War Memorial Auditorium before setting up shop at the three-thousand-person Ryman Auditorium in June 1943.[289]

The former Union Gospel Tabernacle located downtown, the Ryman already was known to locals. Facing growing debts, the auditorium began hosting nonreligious shows, lectures, and sporting events during the early twentieth century. The building's previous history as a gathering place for worshippers facilitated its new identity as a "shrine" to the music played inside. Its decades-long duration as home to *The Opry* attracted entrepreneurs—such as the legendary performer Ernest Tubb, who opened a record shop next door—looking to cash in on the many fans who showed up each week.

What once had been niche "Hillbilly" music grew in respectability. After a 1940 dispute over performance rights with the American Society of Composers, Authors, and Publishers (known as ASCAP), several radio stations led by WSM left the National Association of Broadcasters to establish their own Broadcast Music Incorporated (BMI). The new organization brought together stations specializing in both white and Black music, which established a framework for marketing the roots music that would take the country by storm after World War II: Blues, Rhythm and Blues, Rock n Roll, and Country.[290]

Other behind-the-scenes measures similarly strengthened the place of the music—and with it, Nashville—in American life. In 1944 *Billboard* (which released weekly "charts" ranking record sales) replaced the derogatory "Hillbilly" label with "Folk." Five years later, it divided that category into "Folk," representing the new roots-based music emerging in New York coffee houses and "Country-Western," for the music being played in venues such as the Ryman Auditorium. Technology changed quickly as well, with *The Opry* adding television broadcasting in 1953.

The Postwar Explosion

The Opry's continued growth obscured two postwar trends that would combine to set Nashville on a new path. Nashville entered a period of suburbanization and racial strife while entrepreneurs simultaneously created a business infrastructure that would consolidate Nashville as "America's Music City."

Nashville's suburbanization was typical of metropolitan America. As home to Fisk University, one of the nation's leading Historically Black Colleges and Universities, this period marked profound conflict over racial integration, which was at one and the same time part of a national movement and intensely local. Racial clashes deepened in 1960, when Fisk students organized lunch counter sit-ins downtown. As a result, many whites decided to head for the suburbs, with the city's population falling throughout the decade.

Beyond Nashville's shifting urban morphology, the music business itself had its own unsteady dynamic. As Kosser notes, "The industry waxes and wanes; people get fired and lose their deals; they get hired and find new ones. Songwriters drift from publisher to publisher, and then out of the business altogether. Sometimes it's the peaches, sometimes it's the pits. . . . But every so often, something wonderful breaks through. There's always a chance that something special will change the landscape."[291] In Nashville, it seems, the chances for something special have remained startlingly high.

Simultaneously, pieces in the city's rebirth were being put into place, as would be reflected by extraordinary population growth during the 1970s, from 170,874 to 448,003 by decade's end (a 162.2 percent increase).[292] And a turnaround in the city's music industry began in the 1950s, when the "Big Three" record labels—RCA, Decca, and Columbia—opened recording studios along what would become Music Row, on 16th Avenue near downtown. A decade later, in 1968, local medical entrepreneurs launched the Hospital Corporation of America (HCA), focused initially on the city's university medical faculties at Vanderbilt and elsewhere. HCA would grow into one of the region's largest employers by the twenty-first century.

Even later, the Japanese automaker Nissan opened production facilities nearby, in part to avoid the auto unions firmly established in Detroit. GM and auto parts manufacturer Bridgestone would follow, making Middle Tennessee one of North America's premier car-producing regions. The illustrious Gibson Guitar Company relocated its headquarters to Nashville in 1984. Those businesses, in turn, attracted numerous *Fortune* 500 companies to open offices in Nashville.

The medical and automotive companies would not, in and of themselves, have transformed Nashville into a global city. Humana has remade Louisville into a major medical center and BMW's Spartanburg, South Carolina, plant is among the biggest anywhere. Neither city has claims to global city status. However, because of music, Nashville is no longer just one among many medium-sized American cities. More specifically, what happened to its music industry during the 1950s and 1960s set the city on a new path.

The WSM disc jockey David Cobb first proclaimed Nashville "Music City USA" in a moment of local boosterism in 1950.[293] This claim had some merit, given the growing broadcasting domination of *The Opry*. But many of the pieces that would come to legitimize the claim were still absent at the time.

The Birth of Music Row and the Rise of Music City

Nashville already was supporting small recording studios coming out of World War II, such as Castle Studio. These ventures depended on the technical knowledge of the behind-the-scenes employees at WSM and *The Opry*.[294] This changed when, in the early 1950s, WSM prohibited its employees from taking outside jobs. The engineers running the Castle Studio decided they were better off returning to the WSM fold, thereby forcing the closure of the single noteworthy recording studio in town.

Where some saw peril, others saw opportunity. Owen Bradley seized the moment to head out on his own. Owen joined his brother Harold, a session musician who also was president of the American Federation of Musicians Local 257, to launch their own studio. In the process, they founded Nashville's famous Music Row, along the little houses that lined 16th and 17th avenues south. Today, as Kosser records, the area houses recording studios, music publishing companies, record companies, management companies, and all the other supporting businesses that make the commercial music business run.[295] The Bradley brothers essentially invented Music City.

Kosser adds another important insight when he observes that "the men and women of Music Row are not like other people. They are gamblers. Many of them have no sense at all, or they would have chosen a more sensible way to make a living! Almost all of them came to town without knowing anyone, fully aware that in a year or two they might be slouching home all tuck-tailed and the people they grew up with laughing at them for having had the nerve to believe they could make it."[296] Nashville is fortunate that these gamblers placed their bets along the Music Road three-quarters of a century ago.

Recognizing that whatever recording being done by the large labels in Nashville required bringing in equipment on a temporary basis, Bradley decided to invest in his own top-flight permanent recording studio. Joining with his brother Harold, Grady Martin, Bob Moore, Hank Garland, and Buddy Harman (later collectively known as Nashville's "A-Team"), Bradley built a permanent studio in a Quonset hut that he constructed next to his house.[297]

In 1942, the Chicago-based song writer Fred Rose teamed up with the Hillbilly singer Roy Acuff to promote and publish songwriters and performers.[298] Along the way, they picked up Hank Williams as their client and hit the big time.

For whatever reason, Rose and Acuff did not trust Castle Studio to record Williams and arranged for his first records to be recorded in Cincinnati. Seeing the success of the Bradley studio, they lobbied RCA to build its own studio in town. Acuff teamed up with the now-legendary RCA producer Steve Sholes to launch Studio B in 1957. That workspace was beloved for its acoustics and production quality. Indeed, between 1956 and its closing in 1977, 60 percent of all titles on the *Billboard* country chart began in Studio B.[299] Musicians recorded an estimated 47,000 songs, including Chet Atkins, David Bowie, Johnny Mathis, Roger Miller, Willie Nelson, Dolly Parton, Elvis Presley, Charlie Pride, and Porter Wagoner. RCA eventually would open the larger RCA Studio A as well.

Other record labels—including Decca—followed suit, turning 16th Avenue into "Music Row." This hub proved decisive for the Nashville music industry. As Kosser notes, "Despite all of the studios, record labels, booking agencies, publicity companies, radio stations, and other music organizations that make up the Nashville music business, Music Row is first and foremost a place where songs are written and published. Most people on Music Row regard songwriting as a noble calling."[300] That sensibility and the neighborhood's unprepossessing atmosphere made it a first port of call for new musicians and writers coming to town. Arriving at Nashville with big dreams, hundreds of artists simply made the rounds on Music Row until they struck gold—or struck out.

Nashville now controlled record production as well as marketing. Sixteenth Avenue became a destination for those who sought a musical career, either in front of or behind the microphone and camera. Nearby Belmont College (now University) launched its Mike Curb College of Entertainment and Music Business. Various associated businesses clustered in the area as well.

The country music historian Robert Oermann describes the Row's unique quality. "One thing that makes Music Row unique in the world," he told Kosser, "is that it gives the Nashville music business a sense of community. Unlike Berlin, or London, or New York, or Los Angeles, we have a neighborhood that *is* the music business, and we know each other intimately because of it."[301] When you succeed on Music Row, "the thrill is electric," Kosser reports. "You turn on your car radio every morning when you drive to work, you hear the hits you helped make, and you know that all over the country more than two thousand radio stations are playing *your* music."[302]

Nashville trailed Memphis across the state in total number of recordings issued well into the 1960s. That city's Sam Phillips and Sun Records helped turn Southern Blues and Rhythm and Blues into Rock n Roll, with artists such as Ike Turner, Elvis Presley, Johnny Cash, Roy Orbison, Herry Lee Lewis, Howlin' Wolf, James Cotton, and B. B. King.[303] Nashville put that intrastate rivalry behind it by the mid-1970s.

In 1960, Hattie Louise "Tootsie" Bess purchased Mom's on Broadway, not too far around the corner from the Ryman Auditorium and reopened it as the Orchid Lounge.[304] The place's unpretentious (even "run-down") ambiance and Tootsie's welcoming touch made the lounge into the industry's club house. New arrivals without money came looking for a gig or a writing opportunity; established industry leaders and stars hung out to get the feel for what was happening. This section of Nashville's Broadway soon became "Honky Tonk" Row, chock-a-block full of small bars offering music and cheap beer all day and all night long.

Owsley Manier and Brugh Reynolds opened another important gathering place in 1971 near the Vanderbilt University campus southwest of downtown. Their 200-seat (later 500 seat) Exit/In club proved a beloved hangout for more eccentric types who appreciated smaller venues. Despite changing ownership hands a couple of dozen times, the ambience never changed, with more intellectual songwriters and performers holding forth and developing their own sounds. Specializing in bluegrass, jazz, and stand-up comedy, the Exit/In gave a foot up to the musician-songwriters Rodney Crowell, Guy Clark, and Townes Van Zandt, among many, and to comedians such as Steve Martin.[305]

By the 1980s, Nashville had grown into David Cobb's moniker of "Music City USA." The city had become a go-to place for musicians as diverse as Bob Dylan, the Byrds, Sting, and the Beetles, as well as a legion of Country musicians. The city no longer served just outsiders coming to town to make money. Nashville was generating music—and money—from within; the city was developing its own sound.

The Countrypolitan Nashville Sound

By the late 1950s, record company executives had come to worry about the declining number of radio stations that were playing country and western records.[306] Their music was coming to be seen as a shrinking niche sound, to their dismay. Looking to turn around their reputation—and hence, their commercial value—as something limited to a southern, rural, white audience, they banded together to form the Nashville-based Country Music Association (CMA) in 1958. Their first televised awards show was in 1968. As Kosser notes, "The various members of this young organization rolled up their sleeves and went to work to save the music. They created their own body of demographic research and sales kits and gave pitches and presentations to broadcasters' and advertisers' conventions."[307]

CMA's first success came in the early 1960s: its members convinced *Billboard* to relabel their chart of record sales simply as "Country" rather than "Country and Western" (which itself had added a touch more respectability to the earlier "Hillbilly" label). The rebranding continued with the establishment of the Country Hall of Fame. That venture got off to a rapid start with the induction of Jimmy Rodgers, Hank Williams, and the publisher Fred Rose in its first class. All these efforts represented the consolidation of postwar trends that had been extending the music's reach for several years. Their strategy proved brilliant. Neither the Country Music industry nor Nashville have ever looked back.

Simultaneously, the producers Owen Bradley and Chet Atkins experimented with a new sound in their studios.[308] As Kosser observes, "The music coming out of Nashville in the late '50s and early '60s sounded unique. It sounded *refreshing*. The songwriters wrote with passion. The musicians were creative, not scripted. The artists—well, the artists were *different*." Bradley, who had become head of Decca's Nashville office in 1958, and Atkins at RCA, embraced this new sound.[309]

Nashville studios began replacing hick-sounding "fiddles" with more stylish-sounding violins; they soften the raucous piano lines of the past and turned down the back sounds. This new "sophisticated" (some critics might say "domesticated") sound made the music more palatable to larger audiences. It would become known as the "Nashville Sound."

Beyond changing the music, Bradley and Atkins recordings revealed their studio's heightened technical capacity. The Music Row workplaces became the go-to recording studios for top artists across multiple genres from country to rock to folk, from Gospel to Contemporary Christian music. These collaborations led to cross-over albums such as Ray Charles's 1962 *Country and Western* album and Johnny Cash's multiple efforts to reach jazz, folk, and rock markets.[310]

Nashville's reach expanded as the divisions among genres—once tightly enforced by the *Billboard* charts and radio program formats—became ever more porous. By the mid-1960s, the city and its region were home to 250 music publishers, two dozen record companies, and a burgeoning live music scene.[311] The music industry employed some 5,000 Nashvillians at the time and brought tens of millions of dollars to town. Few cities anywhere offered as many opportunities for back-up musicians, songwriters, and technicians. The city was no longer just about the stars.

As the CMA's rebranding took hold nationwide, a new sound began entering the American cultural mainstream. "Hillbilly" had been transformed into "Countrypolitan," with a devoted following from megacities such as New York and Los Angeles to small towns such as Castle Hayne, NC.

Robert Altman's bold yet chaotic 1975 film *Nashville* captured the ambition of this revived country music scene.[312] In addition to garnering five Oscar nominations, the film is perhaps most notable for capturing the possibility of a nonlawyer winning the US presidency on a platform no more detailed than the candidate not being an attorney. A year later, proud Georgia peanut farmer Jimmy Carter won a trip to the White House on pretty much the same message.

From *The Opry* to Opryland, and Back

Every Saturday night from 1943 until 1974, WSM's *Grand Old Opry* broadcast some forty acts live from the Ryman Auditorium between 6:30 and midnight.[313] This frenetic pace gave live audiences at the "Mother Church of Country Music" more entertainment than anywhere else. The parade of performers allowed radio audiences time to tune in and out as their circumstances allowed. The format left program space for newcomers to give it a go, alongside some of the music's biggest names. Thousands of music pilgrims made their way to Fifth Avenue North to join the fun. They spilled out into nearby eateries, drinking halls, and music clubs, bringing life to an otherwise aging downtown.

The old hall began to show wear and tear, as did the surrounding area.[314] Rebranding the music to make it more respectable required rebranding its physical presence. The music's corporate overseers longed for a larger, more reputable look. By the 1970s, they had raised $65 million to build a country music amusement park in the suburbs, complete with a state-of-the-art auditorium seating 4,400 fans, a 615-room hotel to put them up, and plenty of other wholesome amusements to keep them occupied—and spending money—when the music stopped.

Such tightly controlled spaces were becoming de rigeur as the country seemed to be spinning out of control during the Vietnam War, the Civil Rights Movement, political assassinations, and rising crime. For all that Country music claimed to be All-American, those who controlled its fate wanted to close out as much of an unsavory America as possible.

The old hall was packed when *The Opry* signed off for the last time at Ryman Auditorium. The next broadcast, from the new Opryland Auditorium, included President Richard Nixon playing "Happy Birthday" on the piano for his wife, serenading her with "My Irish Wild Rose," and leading the audience in a rendition of "God Bless America."[315]

Just as Nixon himself was in deep trouble at the time, as the Watergate Scandal picked up steam, WSM's corporate leadership should not have been as self-confident as they seemed. Not everyone was pleased with letting the old theater go, including some of the music's biggest names. Nostalgia lost out to profit, at least at first. The new suburban Opryland was a great success, bringing in enormous profits from the very beginning.

The old Ryman languished, slowly deteriorating in a decaying downtown that was typical of urban America at the time. The community began to organize once WSM president Irving Waugh let slip his plans to demolish the old hall and build a replacement "Little Church of Opryland." Roy Acuff and other well-established stars joined with hundreds of others to save the old building. First, they secured a designation as a National Historic Landmark to stave off demolition; then, over the next twenty years, they raised the funds to undertake major renovations. Periodic one-off shows reminded everyone of how special the Ryman was, with its incomparable acoustics and its audiences seated at the performers' feet.[316] *The Opry* returned for a benefit show in October 1998, and the stage has been active ever since.

The revitalized Ryman Auditorium anchored the newly energized downtown core, embracing Broadway's Honky Tonk Row, the vast Country Music Hall of Fame complex, the National Hockey

League arena, the Tennessee Performing Arts Center, and the Schermerhorn Symphony Center. The surrounding late-nineteenth- and early-twentieth-century buildings proved popular with buyers looking for an urban experience. Downtown became the anchor for the expanding metropolitan region rather than the hole at its center. With its music business, its tourist industry focused on Opryland and other music venues, its recording studios and back offices, the expanding health care sector, automotive manufacturing, and financial services, Greater Nashville has emerged from the COVID-19 pandemic of the early 2020s better placed for success than almost any other American metropolitan region.

From Flyover City to Destination

Americans often speak derisively of the cities west of the Appalachians and east of the Rockies as "flyover cities." The "bicoastal" set of well-off elites might enjoy looking at these communities from the window of an airplane, but they would never think of visiting one. Most state capitals fall into this category, as Nashville would have a century ago, if there had been coast-to-coast flights to fly over it.

During the past century, Nashville has evolved from a medium-sized flyover city of no particular distinction among a couple of dozen quite indifferent state capitals to one of the country's fastest-growing and most interesting cities —a true destination. The travel writer Leena Kollar put it this way in May 2017 on the *Culture Trip* blog: "There are major US cities, such as New York City on the East Coast and Los Angeles on the West Coast, that attract millions of visitors each year. In the South, there's Nashville. More than just a country music hot spot, Nashville is a 'small town trapped in a big city' that makes tourists curious about all that it has to offer."[317] This view has been shared by scores of travel writers hundreds of times over the past decade.

This transformation accelerates with each passing year. How has this happened? This dynamism rests first and foremost on the city's music industry. In the earlier cases examined here the performing arts shifted in response to the cities changing around them. In the case of Nashville, it is music that made the town.

Chapter 7

Concluding Observations

The five case studies presented in this volume reveal how the lives of cities and the evolving performing arts interact with one another. Stages shift as cities and communities change, and vice versa. The preceding chapters have revealed how growing cities have nurtured the emergence of new performing arts—as was the case with the growth of performance dance in Montreal—and have reflected a growing maturation of urbanization, as was the case with grassroots theater movements in Toronto and Washington. They also highlight the interaction between new urban functions and expanding performing arts, as happened in Kyiv after Ukrainian independence. Together, they reveal the interactive relationship between urban and artistic change across at least four dimensions: the economic, the political, the social, and the technological.

The Nashville story accentuates how an expanding arts scene—in this case, the growth of the country music business—can drive the extension of a city's reputation and economic power. One of many undistinguished American state capital cities a century ago, Nashville is now a global destination for music fans. Nashville's metropolitan economy has fed from this development to attract new industries, such as health care and automobile manufacturing. The city and its region have ridden this virtuous cycle for several decades as Nashville has become one of North America's major corporate centers.

Perhaps less readily apparent, the same synergies between the arts and the urban economy are visible in the transformations that have taken place over the past three-quarters-of-a-century in Washington and Toronto. As both cities developed into metropolitan powerhouses during the late twentieth century, their economies created audiences with knowledge, curiosity, and incomes to support the arts. The arts, in turn, have become increasingly important economic sectors accelerating their regional dynamism. Some estimates suggest that the arts account for around 3 per cent of the Washington, D.C. metropolitan economy creating over 200,000 jobs with total household expenditures on the arts nearly five times the national average.[318] With nearly 200,000 employees, the culture sector provides more employment and contributes more to Ontario's GDP than the energy industry, agriculture, forestry and mining sectors combined.[319]

The relationship between the arts and urban politics is more visible. As we have seen in the rise of performance dance in Montreal, the ebb and flow of artistic innovation and institutional security tracked that of the battles over Quebec sovereignty. On the one hand, dance transcended the city's linguistic divides; on the other, dance companies gained greater attention when the battle over independence rose, as around the referendums in 1980 and 1995.[320] Similarly, theater became a powerful form of expression during the drive for civil rights in Washington.[321]

The transformation of Kyiv's theater scene over the past three decades is connected directly to the political forces which established Ukrainian sovereignty when the Soviet Union collapsed. A search for distinctive Ukrainian theatrical roots in earlier times has combined with the challenges of theater in wartime to elevate Kyiv's theater scene to one worthy of international attention.[322]

Each of the cases except for that focusing on Kyiv are set during the arrival of the Baby Boomer generation, which created a lucrative market for mass consumption of popular culture. More micro-level social change became important for how the performing arts shifted in response to demographic changes in cities themselves. The massive expansion of immigrant communities in Toronto and Washington attracted thousands of new residents for whom the arts were accepted as important aspects of the good life. Generations of city dwellers who were digital natives from birth created striking opportunities for the performing arts to head off in new directions. Those arriving in Nashville searching for a foothold in the music industry altered how everyone in Nashville viewed their town.

Finally, many of the stories presented here highlight the transformative role of new technology for the arts. Radio and television were fundamental in nurturing the new dance community in Montreal and the course of Nashville's music scene. New recording technologies elevated Nashville's sound stages to new heights internationally. The internet has brought what is happening on wartime stages in Kyiv to international audiences in real time. Social media permitted fans to track their favorite performers and companies in Washington and Toronto throughout the COVID-19 pandemic.

Beyond identifying these broad trends, the chapters track each story in detail to communicate how these interactions play out. While none of the stories are identical, they all share general characteristics. The arrival of new generations of residents and businesses creates the disposable wealth required to support the performing arts. Residents representing differing communities became interested in diverse art forms. Over time, an economic and communal base for specific art forms solidifies. Growth is not continuous, but the long-term effects of that expansion reshape the urban cultural landscape.

If Montreal was not a center of performance dance a half-century ago, it is now; Toronto has become a resilient theater community; and Washington, one of American theater's hotspots. The broadening of the performance arts in Kyiv accompanying that city's new status as an international capital will continue; and Nashville will remain "America's Music City" well into the twenty-first century.

Together, these stories reveal how the arts mobilize emotions—be they about specific performers and art forms, or communal identities and divisions. Since the first humans stood by a campfire and sang, danced, and recited epic tales, the arts have expressed our collective aspirations and most profound disappointments. They reaffirm our innate social nature, extending that primeval campfire into our own era.

Electronic—and now digital—media have profoundly undermined the sense of community nurtured by live performance. Engaging artistic creativity has become ever more atomistical. These transformations encourage us to view the performing arts as increasingly obsolete and irrelevant to our lives.

Embracing the digital age as a new world brought ex nihilo into reality is a mistake. How we engage with one another and with our own yearnings for creative expression evolve; they do not cease. As our behavior during the recent COVID-19 epidemic underscores, humans crave social interactions; and few forces are more powerful in supporting such connections than those unleased at live performances. The arts still matter to us individually and collectively; and they interact with broader societal trends as they do.

Cities still matter too. Computer screens and social media devices are not substitutes for the serendipitous propinquity of urban spaces. Cities offer energy efficiencies that are becoming increasingly important in a time of climate change. As the COVID-19 shutdowns taught is, humans as social animals crave the communal experiences provided by the arts (and sports).

Looking to the future, the relationships between changing cities and their shifting stages is not winding down. Those who are concerned about the arts and about urban communities would do well to keep an eye on the variety of exchanges between the two that have been highlighted here.

Perhaps hard-nosed observers consider the arts as little more than white noise. If so, they miss a much larger story. The performing arts, as communal and social activities, bring humans together in all their agreements and disagreements. They express some of the deepest human emotions and, in response, intensify our innermost passions. What happens when performers meet their audiences signals how we see ourselves and our futures; and how we like what we see, or not. A night at the theater, the concert hall, or a night club is always about more than an entertaining backdrop to the political and economic forces that really matter.

About the Author

Blair A. Ruble has written widely on the relationship between the performing arts and community, including several monographs: *The Arts of War: Year One & Year Two* (2023, 2024), *Proclaiming Presence from the Washington Stage* (2021), *The Muse of Urban Delirium* (2017), and *Washington's U Street* (2010). He also is the author of a trilogy of works examining the fate of Russian provincial cities during the twentieth century: *Leningrad* (1990), *Money Sings!* (1995), and *Second Metropolis* (2001). Other books include *Creating Diversity Capital* (2005), and *Soviet Trade Unions* (1981). He has held several positions at Washington's Woodrow Wilson International Center for Scholars including Vice President for Programs and Director of the Kennan Institute. A native of New York, Blair Ruble graduated from the University of North Carolina, Chapel Hill and earned his doctoral degree from the University of Toronto.

Notes

WTCR— Washington Theater Club Records, 1952-79, Special Collections Research Center, George Washington University, Washington, D.C.

Introduction

1 Graham Robb, *Victor Hugo* (New York: W. W. Norton, 1997).
2 Micheline Milot, "The Priest-Ridden Province? Politics and Religion in Quebec," in *Quebec Questions. Quebec Studies for the Twenty-First Century*, ed. Stéphan Gervais, Christopher Kirkey, and Jarret Rudy (Toronto: Oxford University Press Canada, 2011), 123–36.
3 Taras Grescoe, *Sacré Blues. An Unsentimental Journey Through Québec* (Toronto: Macfarlane Walter & Ross, 2000), 23–76.
4 Iro Valaskakis Tembeck, "Dancing in Montreal. Seeds of a Choreographic History," *Studies in Dance History* 5, no. 2 (1994): 1–146, at 1–10.
5 Among many discussions of this process, see Jocelyn Maclure, "Quebec's Culture War: Two Conceptions of Quebec Identity," in *Quebec Questions*, ed. Gervais, Kirkey, and Rudy, 153–67; and Michael D. Behiels, Prelude to Quebec's Quiet Revolution: Liberalism vs Neo-Nationalism 1945–60 (McGill-Queen's Press, 1985); as well as Donald Cuccioletta and Martin Lubin. "The Quebec Quiet Revolution: A Noisy Evolution," *Quebec Studies* 36, no. 1 (2003): 125–38.
6 Tembeck, "Dancing in Montreal," 3–6; Andrew Oxenham with Michael Crabb, *Dance Today in Canada* (Toronto: Simon & Pierre, 1977), 7–14.
7 Tembeck, "Dancing in Montreal," 3–4; Iro Valaskakis Tembeck, "Politics and Dance in Montreal, 1940s to 1980s: The Imaginary Maginot Line between Anglophone and Francophone Dancers," in *Canadian Dance: Visions and Stories*, ed. Selma Landen Odom and Mary Jane Warner (Toronto: Dance Collection Danse Press, 2004), 271–86.

8   Jacob E. Cooke, "The Compromise of 1790," *William and Mary Quarterly* 27 (October 1970): 523–45.
9   Lin-Manuel Miranda, Jeremy McCarter, *Hamilton: The Revolution* (New York: Grand Central, 2016), Act II, Song 5.
10 David L. Lewis, *District of Columbia: A Bicentennial History* (Nashville: American Association for State and Local History; and New York: W. W. Norton, 1976), 7–15.
11 Constance McLaughlin Green, *The Secret City: A History of Race Relations in the Nation's Capital* (Princeton, NJ: Princeton University Press, 1967); Silvio Bedini, *The Life of Benjamin Banneker* (New York: Charles Scribner's Sons, 1972).
12 Steven J. Diner, *Democracy, Federalism, and the Governance of the Nation's Capital, 1790–1974,* Studies in DC History and Public Policy 10 (Washington, DC: Center for Applied Research and Urban Policy, University of the District of Columbia, 1987). 7–8, 13–14.
13 Kate Masur, *An Example for All the Land: Emancipation and the Struggle over Equality in Washington, DC* (Chapel Hill: University of North Carolina Press, 2010); Chris Myers Asch and George Derek Musgrove, *Chocolate City: A History of Race and Democracy in the Nation's Capital* (Chapel Hill: University of North Carolina Press, 2017).
14 Howard Gillette Jr., *Between Justice and Beauty: Race, Planning, and the Failure of Urban Policy in Washington, DC* (Baltimore: Johns Hopkins University Press, 1995).
15 Derek Hyra and Sabiyha Prince, eds., *Capital Dilemma: Growth and Inequality in Washington, DC* (New York: Routledge, 2016).
16 Derek S. Hyra, *Race, Class and Politics in the Cappuccino City* (Chicago: University of Chicago Press, 2017).
17 Washington Theater Club Records, 1952–79, Special Collections Research Center, George Washington University, Washington.
18 Harold Kaplan, *Urban Political Systems: A Functional Analysis of Metro Toronto* (New York: Columbia University Press, 1967); David A. Wilson, ed., *The Orange Order in Canada* (Dublin: Four Courts Press, 2007).
19 John Lorine, Michael McClelland, Ellen Scheinberg and Tatum Taylor, eds., *The Ward: The Life and Loss of Toronto's First Immigrant Neighborhood* (Toronto: Coach House Books, 2015).

20 Nick Mount, *Arrival. The Story of CanLit* (Toronto: House of Anansi Press, 2017).
21 Leopold Infeld, *Quest: An Autobiography* (Providence: American Mathematical Society / Chelsea Publishing, 1980), 324.
22 Ruth A. Fager, *Sweatshop Strife: Class, Ethnicity, and Gender in the Jewish Labour Movement of Toronto, 1900–1939* (Toronto: University of Toronto Press, 1992); Erna Paris, *Jews: An Account of Their Experience in Canada* (Toronto: Macmillan of Canada, 1980); Shmuel Mayer Shapiro, *The Rise of the Toronto Jewish Community* (Toronto: Now & Then Books, 2010).
23 Cyril Levitt and William Shaffir, *The Riots at Christie Pits* (Toronto: Lester & Orpen Dennys, 1987).
24 Eric Arthur, *Toronto. No Mean City* (Toronto: University of Toronto Press, 1986); Albert Rose, *Governing Metropolitan Toronto: A Social and Political Analysis* (Berkeley: University of California Press, 1972).
25 Robert F. Harney, eds., *Gathering Place: Peoples and Neighborhoods of Toronto, 1834–1945* (Toronto: Multicultural History Society of Ontario, 1985).
26 Paul Anisef and Michael Lamphier, eds., *The World in a City* (Toronto: University of Toronto Press, 2003).
27 This period is covered by Michael F. Hamm, *Kiev. A Portrait, 1800–1917* (Princeton, NJ: Princeton University Press, 1996).
28 A quick overview of the city's twentieth-century history is given by Katya Cengel, "The 20th-Century History Behind Russia's Invasion of Ukraine," *Smithsonian Magazine*, March 4, 2022.
29 Wendy Morgan Lower, "From Berlin to Baby Yar: The Nazi War Against the Jews, 1941–1944," *Journal of Religion & Society* 9 (2007): 1–14.
30 Andrew Wilson, *The Ukrainians: Unexpected Nation* (New Haven, CT: Yale University Press, 2000), 234–52.
31 Serhii Plokhy, *Chernobyl. The History of a Nuclear Catastrophe* (New York, Basic Books, 2018).
32 This account is based on interviews and conversations with several eyewitnesses to these events.
33 Campbell Gibson, *Population of the 100 Largest Cities and Other Urban Places in the US, 1790 to 1990* (Washington, DC: US Census Bureau, 1998).

34 Cynthis Cumfer, *Separate Peoples, on Land: The Minds of Cherokees, Blacks and Whites on the Tennessee Frontier* (Chapel Hill: University of North Carolina Press, 2007).
35 *Nashville–Davidson County Metropolitan Government: Selected Economic Characteristics: 2007–2011* (Washington, DC: US Census Bureau, 2013).
36 Dayton Duncan and Ken Burns, *Country Music. An Illustrated History* (New York: Alfred A. Knopf, 2019), 19–28.
37 Duncan and Burns, 92–99.
38 William U. Eiland, *Nashville's Mother Church: The History of the Ryman Auditorium* (Nashville: Abe Books, 1992).

Montreal

39 Micheline Milot, "The Priest-Ridden Province? Politics and Religion in Quebec," in *Quebec Questions. Quebec Studies for the Twenty-First Century*, ed. Stéphan Gervais, Christopher Kirkey, and Jarret Rudy (Toronto: Oxford University Press Canada, 2011), 123–36.
40 Iro Tembeck, *Dancing in Montreal: Seeds of a Choreographic History* (Oak Creek, WI: Society of Dance History Scholars, 1994), 22–23; Karen Stanworth, "Re-Placing Performance: The Inter-Media Practice of François Sullivan," in *Canadian Dance: Visions and Stories*, ed. Selma Landen Odom and Mary Jane Warner (Toronto: Dance Collection Danse Press, 2004), 329–38; Robert Enright, "A Woman for All Seasons: An Interview with Françoise Sullivan," *BorderCrossings*, issue 106, May 2008; Dan Taylor, "Refus Global by Paul-Émile Borduas," www.dantaylor.com/pages/frenchrefusglobal.html.
41 Iro Valaskakis Tembeck, "Françoise Sullivan," in *Encyclopedia of Theatre Dance in Canada / Encyclopédie de la Danse Théâtrale au Canada*, ed. Susan Macpherson (Toronto: Dance Collection Danse Press, 2000), 563–65.
42 Allana Lindgren, "François Sullivan: An Introduction," in *Canadian Dance*, ed. Odom and Warner, 10–19.
43 Linde Howe-Beck, "Jeanne Renaud," in *Encyclopedia*, ed. Macpherson, 482–87.
44 Geraldine Anthony, *Stage Voices: Twelve Canadian Playwrights*

Talk About Their Lives and Work (Toronto: Doubleday Canada, 1978), xix–xxi.
45 Nick Mont, *Arrival: The Story of CanLit* (Toronto: Anasi, 2017), 123–27, 181–94; Cheryl Smith, "Stepping Out: A New Look at Canada's Early Ballet Companies, 1939 to 1960," in *Canadian Dance*, ed. Odom and Warner, 197–223, at 216–20.
46 Roger Lemelin," Canadian Writers Website, www. collectionscamada/gc.ca/writers/027005-2000-e.html.
47 Anthony, *Stage Voices*, xxi–xxiii.
48 Iro Valaskakis Tembeck, "Maurice Lacasse Morenoff, Carmen Sierra Morenoff," in *Encyclopedia*, ed. Macpherson, 394–95; Howe-Beck, "Jeanne Renaud," in *Encyclopedia*, ed. Macpherson, 482–84.
49 Tembeck, *Dancing in Montreal*, 11–17.
50 Tembeck, "Maurice Lacasse Morenoff," 395; Pierre Lapointe, "Three Intrepid Montreal Dancers of the 1940s and 1950s," in *Canadian Dance*, ed. Odom and Warner, 287–95.
51 Tembeck, *Dancing in Montreal*, 17–19.
52 Grant Strate, "Canadian Dance in Progress: A Personal View," in *Canadian Dance*, ed. Odom and Warner, 21–32.
53 Iro Valaskakis Tembeck, "Gérald Crevier," in *Encyclopedia*, ed. Macpherson, 394–95.
54 Linde Howe-Beck, "Ludmilla Chiriaeff," in *Encyclopedia*, ed. Macpherson, 118–21.
55 Smith, "Stepping Out," 214–19.
56 Iro Valaskakis Tembeck, "Politics and Dance in Montreal, 1940s to 1980s: The Imaginary Maginot Line between Anglophone and Francophone Dancers," in *Canadian Dance*, ed. Odom and Warner, 278–80.
57 Smith, "Stepping Out," 197–223; Katherine Cornell, "The Ballet Problem: The Kirstein-Buckle Ballet Survey for the Canada Council," in *Canadian Dance*, ed. Odom and Warner, 225–38.
58 Tembeck, *Dancing in Montreal*, 23–25.
59 Tembeck, 25–28.
60 Tembeck, 28–32.
61 Smith, "Stepping Out."
62 Cornell, "Ballet Problem."
63 Smith, "Stepping Out," 221.

64 "Les Grands Ballets Canadiens de Montréal," in *The Canadian Encyclopedia*, www.thecanadianencyclopedia.ca/.
65 "Les Grands Ballets Canadiens."
66 Michael Gauvreau, *Catholic Origins of Quebec's Quiet Revolution, 1931–1970* (Montreal: McGill-Queen's Press, 2005); Michael D. Behiels, *Prelude to Quebec's Quiet Revolution: Liberalism vs Neo-Nationalism, 1945-60* (Montreal: McGill-Queen's Press, 1985).
67 Sylvain Schryburt, "Quebec Theatre: New Dynamics between the Local and International," in *Quebec Questions. Quebec Studies for the Twenty-First Century*, 2nd edition, ed. Stéphan Gervais, Christopher Kirkey and Jarret Rudy (New York: Oxford University Press, 2016), 443–55; Gregory J. Reid, "Performing Anglo Quebec: The Myth of Solitudes and Merging Anglo-Québécois Subject," *Journal of Canadian Studies* 46, no. 3 (2012): 105–27.
68 Paul-Andre Linteau, *The History of Montreal: The Story of a Great North American City*, trans. Peter MacCambridge (Montreal: Baraka Books, 2013), 166.
69 Andrew Oxenham with Michael Crabb, *Dance Today in Canada* (Toronto: Simon & Pierre, 1977), 27–28.
70 Howe-Beck, "Ludmilla Chiriaeff."
71 Linde Howe-Beck, "Les Grands Ballets Canadiens," in *Encyclopedia*, ed. Macpherson, 241–45.
72 Tembeck, *Dancing in Montreal*, 38–39.
73 Tembeck, "Politics and Dance," in *Canadian Dance*, ed. Odom and Warner, 279.
74 Jo Leslie, "Le Groupe de la Place Royale," in *Encyclopedia*, ed. Macpherson, 250–53.
75 Tembeck, *Dancing in Montreal*, 47–48.
76 Lai-Ling Lee, "Peter Boneham," in *Encyclopedia*, ed. Macpherson, 89–91.
77 Leslie, "Le Groupe," in *Encyclopedia*, ed. Macpherson.
78 "Le Groupe de la Place Royale," in *The Canadian Encyclopedia*, www. thecanadianencyclopedia.ca/.
79 "Le Groupe Dance Lab," in *The Canadian Encyclopedia*, www.thecanadianencyclopedia.ca/.
80 "Le Groupe Dance Lab."
81 Tembeck, *Dancing in Montreal*, 58–61.

82 Tembeck, "Politics and Dance," in *Canadian Dance*, ed. Odom and Warner, 280–82.
83 "Le Groupe Nouvelle Aire," in *The Canadian Encyclopedia*, www.thecanadianencyclopedia.ca/; Martine Époque, *Les coulisses de la nouvelle danse au Québec, Le Groupe Nouvelle Aire en mémoires, 1968–1982* (Sanite-Foy: Presses de l'Université du Québec, 1999); Oxenham with Crabb, *Dance Today*, 30–35.
84 Iro Valaskakis Tembeck, "Martine Époque," in *Encyclopedia*, ed. Macpherson, 178–80.
85 Aline Gélinas, "Paul-André Fortier," in *Encyclopedia*, ed. Macpherson, 198–200.
86 Kathryn Greenaway, "Ginette Laurin," in *Encyclopedia*, ed. Macpherson, 330–32.
87 Linde Howe-Beck, "Eva von Gencsy," in *Encyclopedia*, ed. Macpherson, 611–13.
88 Howe-Beck.
89 Howe-Beck.
90 Lys Stevens, "Eva von Gencsy (1924–2013)," *Dance Current*, December 4, 2013.
91 Tembeck, "Politics and Dance," in *Canadian Dance*, ed. Odom and Warner, 284.
92 Kathryn Greenaway, "Éduard Lock," in *Encyclopedia*, ed. Macpherson, 357–59.
93 Victor Swoboda, "La La La Human Steps Is No More, Édouard Lock Announces," *Montreal Gazette*, September 2, 2015.
94 Tembeck, *Dancing in Montreal*, 86–92.
95 Linde Howe-Beck, "École de danse contemporaine de Montréal, in *The Canadian Encyclopedia*, www. thecanadianencyclopedia.ca/.
96 Kathryn Greenaway, "Linda Rabin," in *Encyclopedia*, ed. Macpherson, 469–71.
97 Samantha Mehra, "Candace Loubert (1947–2011)," *Dance Current*, November 23, 2011.
98 Linde Howe-Beck, "Daniel Soulièrs," in *Encyclopedia*, ed. Macpherson, 543–45.
99 Gélinas, "Paul-André Fortier," in *Encyclopedia*, ed. Macpherson, 198–200.
100 Tembeck, *Dancing in Montreal*, 86.

101 Christopher Jones, "Popular Music in Quebec," in *Quebec Questions*, ed. Gervais, Kirkey, and Rudy, 212–26; Sylvain Schryburt, "Quebec Theatre: New Dynamics between the Local and the International," in *Quebec Questions*, 443–54; Thomas A. Cummins-Russell and Norma M. Rantisi, "Networks and Place in Montreal's Independent Music Industry," *Canadian Geographer* 56, no. 1 (2012): 80–97.

102 François Sullivan, "Dance and Hope," in *Canadian Dance*, ed. Odom and Warner, 11–18, at 16.

Washington

103 See, e.g., Leo Sullivan, "Helen Morgan Film Strictly for Buffs Strictly for Film Buffs," *Washington Post*, October 4, 1957; and Richard L. Coe, "'J.B.' Has 'Em Talking," *Washington Post*, November 12, 1961.

104 Richard L. Coe, "A Hideous Fact of Life," *Washington Post*, May 4, 1961; "News Notes on Dance," *Washington Post*, May 7, 1961.

105 "Theater Club Announces Plays, Appoints New Artistic Director," *Washington Post*, August 8, 1965.

106 Megan Rosenfeld, "Theater Club Appointments," *Washington Post*, September 14, 1972.

107 See, e.g., James Lardner, "Davey Marlin-Jones, Director," *Washington Post*, August 5, 1979; Mary Lynn Kotz, "Marvella Bayh: Her Story of Courage," *Boston Globe*, December 9, 1979; Joe Brown, "A Broadway Baby, If Just for One Night," *Washington Post*, August 14, 1987; John Carmody, "The TV Column," *Washington Post*, December 28, 1987.

108 Richard L. Coe, "Mayor to Uphold Tradition," *Washington Post*, April 10, 1969; Richard L. Coe, "Theater Club a Winner," *Washington Post*, April 12, 1969. The award to Davey Marlin-Jones was made before Arena Stage's Zelda Fichandler received the same award; Richard L. Coe, "The Margo Jones Award," *Washington Post*, March 18, 1971; Richard L. Coe, "Margo Jones Award," *Washington Post*, March 9, 1972; "Honors for Zelda and Arena," *Washington Post*, May 16, 1972.

109 Adam Bernstein, "Director Davey Marlin-Jones Dies," *Washington Post*, March 4, 2004.

110 See, e.g., Meryle Secrest, "Teens Get in the Act," *Washington Post*, August 12, 1962; Leo Sullivan, "Comedy and Drama in Abyssinia Sands," *Washington Post*, August 16, 1962; "Grimm—but Happy," *Washington Post*, August 17, 1962; "Bremertown Musicians," *Washington Post*, August 26, 1962; "Special Events for Small Fry," *Washington Post*, December 22, 1964; Richard L. Coe, "Theater as a Hobby," *Washington Post*, March 28, 1965; Richard L. Coe, "Convent Days Here Again," *Washington Post*, April 8, 1965; Richard L. Coe, "'Born Free' Is Rare Film," *Washington Post*, April 7, 1966; "Especially for Children This Week," *Washington Post*, April 10, 1966; "'Brigadoon' Brought to Lisner," *Washington Post*, April 10, 1966; "Places to Take Your Children," *Washington Post*, April 17, 1966; "Bulletin Board: Beckett Continues, Filmers Meet," *Washington Post*, April 17, 1966; "Theater Promptbook," *Washington Post*, April 14, 1968; "Theater Seminars Scheduled in La Plata," *Washington Post*, June 16, 1968; Richard L. Coe, "Hughes Once Owned Andes," *Washington Post*, July 24, 1968. Adam Bernstein, "Director Davey Marlin-Jones Dies," *Washington Post*, March 4, 2004. See, e.g., Secrest, "Teens."

111 See, e.g., Richard L. Coe, "Andre Tahon's Puppets at the National Theater," *Washington Post*, December 23, 1971; Meryle Secrest, "Brown's Puppet Show," *Washington Post*, October 30, 1970; Megan Rosenfeld, "Puppet Theater to Close," *Washington Post*, February 3, 1972; Megan Rosenfeld, "Holiday Puppets," *Washington Post*, December 23, 1972; "Carrousel," *Washington Post*, April 13, 1973; Megan Rosenfeld, "Performing Arts Publication," *Washington Post*, April 15, 1973; Megan Rosenfeld, "Puppeteers' New 'Rumpel,'" *Washington Post*, April 16, 1973; "Carrousel," *Washington Post*, April 20, 1973; and Meryle Secrest, "Two Puppet Troupes," *Washington Post*, January 7, 1971.

112 See, e.g., Jean Battey, "Second Ballet Company Budding Here," *Washington Post*, April 22, 1962; Alan M. Kriegsman, "Engrossing Debut Chamber Concert," *Washington Post*, June 12, 1968; Paul Hume, "Pianist Adds 3d Dimension," *Washington Post*, April 22, 1969; Donald McCorkle, "Attractive, Unusual," *Washington Post*, April 29, 1969; Paul Hume, "Symphony Compe-

tition," *Washington Post*, June 24, 1969; Paul Hume, "Concert Presentations Expanding," *Washington Post*, October 28, 1969; Paul Hume, "A New Sound; a New Audience," *Washington Post*, November 21, 1969; "US Composers Honored," *Washington Post*, March 17, 1970; Paul Hume, "Summer Music Season," *Washington Post*, May 19, 1970; Alan M. Kriegsman, "Hazardous Diversification," *Washington Post*, May 26, 1970; Paul Hume, "National Symphony's U.N. Concert," *Washington Post*, October 6, 1970; Paul Hume, "Varese, Crumb, Bartok," *Washington Post*, December 15, 1970; Paul Hume, "Elusive Mozart Score," *Washington Post*, February 21, 1971; Paul Hume, "Theater Chamber Players," *Washington Post*, December 14, 1971; Alan M. Kriegsman, "A Blaze of Glory," *Washington Post*, December 19, 1972; Paul Hume, "The Message of the Requiem," *Washington Post*, January 23, 1973; Paul Hume, "Casals and More Casals," *Washington Post*, May 8, 1973; Alan M. Kriegsman, "Daring and Well Worth It," *Washington Post*, May 15, 1973; Paul Hume, "Music, Music," *Washington Post*, September 9, 1973; Paul Hume, "Chamber Players: Usual Excellence," *Washington Post*, October 2, 1973 John Rockwell, "Leon Fleisher's Other Careers," *New York Times*, July 22, 1979.

113 Geoffrey A. Wolff, "Empty Seats Puzzle Club's Director," *Washington Post*, May 22, 1966.

114 See, e.g., Richard L. Coe, "Tough Hides, Inner Bruises," *Washington Post*, October 24, 1963; Jean Battey, "Repertory Company Does Closeup Ballet," *Washington Post*, March 2, 1964; Jean Battey, "The Dance: Two Troupes to Play Washington on Saturday," *Washington Post*, March 8, 1964; Judith Martin, "Drama for the Kids," *Washington Post*, June 12, 1969; Meryle Secrest, "Brown's Puppet Show," *Washington Post*, October 30, 1970; Richard L. Coe, "'Max Moth' at Ford's Theater," *Washington Post*, November 26, 1970; Richard L. Coe, "'Max Morath at the Turn of the Century' Returns to Ford's," *Washington Post*, December 10, 1970; Alan M. Kriegsman, "Squeals of Approval," *Washington Post*, March 25, 1971; Megan Rosenfeld, "Holiday Puppets," *Washington Post*, December 23, 1972; Megan Rosenfeld, "Puppeteers' New 'Rumpel,'" *Washington Post*, April 16, 1973.

115 William H. Jones, "$300 Million Plan for West End Unveiled," *Washington Post*, May 12, 1973; John B. Williams, "It's Happening in Real Estate: West End: Intown Invitation," *Washington Post*, June 24, 1972; Richard L. Coe, "Washington Theater Club's Plans," *Washington Post*, August 3, 1972.
116 "WTC Production Series," WTCR, boxes 1–22, folders 1–590; box 26, files 649–58.
117 "History-Wentworth Dramatic Effort Prior to Washington Drama Center," WTCR, box 70, folder 1093.
118 "History: Wentworth Dramatic Effort Prior to Washington Drama Center," WTCR, box 70, folder 1093.
119 "Facilities," WTCR, box 70, folder 1094.
120 "Undated, circa 1960: An Appeal," WTCR, box 70, folder 1094.
121 "Summer 1960: 'The Theater,'" WTCR, box 70, folder 1094.
122 "Undated: Playwriting Contest," WTCR, box 70, folder 1094; Richard L. Coe, "Spring Plug for Summer," *Washington Post*, March 25, 1959.
123 See, e.g., Richard L. Coe, "The Monday Night Reading," *Washington Post*, February 28, 1971.
124 "September 20, 1957: Washington Theater Club Board of Directors, Executive Session," WTCR, box 74, folder 1140/41.
125 "Circa 1960: Handwritten Mission Statement," WTCR, box 70, folder 1094.
126 "Production 43, 'Caligula' by Albert Camus, February 15–March 25, 1968," WTCR, box 9, folders 284–91.
127 For further discussion of the Jim Crow era in Washington theater history see Blair A. Ruble, *Proclaiming Presence from the Washington Stage* (Washington, DC: New Academia Press, 2020).
128 For further discussion of the role of the Catholic University faculty in opposing Jim Crow, see Mary Jo Santo Pietro, *Father Hartke: His Life and Legacy to the American Theater* (Washington, DC: Catholic University of America Press, 2002).
129 For a discussion of Arena Stage's history of engagement with race, see Donatella Galella, *America in the Round: Capital, Race, and Nation at Washington, DC's Arena Stage* (Iowa City: University of Iowa Press, 2019).

130 Hollie I. West, "Jazz Event a 'Triumph,'" *Washington Post*, November 18, 1970; Hollie I. West, "Marshall Hawkins in Concert," *Washington Post*, April 12, 1972.

131 "Minutes. Meeting of Washington Theater Club Board of Trustees, February 18, 1971," WCTR, box 75, file 1154.

132 Richard L. Coe, "Lifelike Jets, Robot People," *Washington Post*, July 19, 1963; Richard L. Coe, "Artists to Talk at Theater Club," *Washington Post*, August 4, 1963.

133 Jeannette Smyth, "Fresh Promise of Success," *Washington Post*, June 20, 1972.

134 "Production 7, 'Call Me By My Rightful Name' by Michael Shurtleff, July 11–23, 1961," WCTR, box 1, folders 18–24.

135 Richard L. Coe, "Trees Clutter O-St. 'Forest,'" *Washington Post*, July 14, 1961.

136 Robertson Campbell, "Michael Shurtleff, Casting Director for Broadway and Hollywood, Dies at 86," *New York Times*, February 12, 2007.

137 "Geoffrey Horne Joins 'Merrily' Cast," *New York Times*, November 13, 1981; "Collin Wilcox Paxton Dies at 74; actress was Mayella in 'To Kill a Mockingbird,'" *Los Angeles Times*, October 23, 2009.

138 C. Gerald Fraser, "Bill Gunn, Playwright and Actor, Dies at 54 on Eve of Play Premier," *New York Times*, April 7, 1989.

139 "Production 14, 'Brecht on Brecht' translated by George Tabort, February 27–April 13, 1963," WCTR, box 14, folders 69–77.

140 Richard L. Coe, "Ear Caught By 'Brecht'" *Washington Post*, February 27, 1963.

141 Richard L. Coe, "USIA Films Admirable Lot," *Washington Post*, February 8, 1963; Richard L. Coe, "She Who Gets Slapped," *Washington Post*, February 21, 1963; "Ballad by Brecht," *Washington Post*, March 6, 1963; "Five Plus Two," *Washington Post*, March 10, 1963; "A Night Off," *Washington Post*, April 1, 1963; "Brecht Reader," *Washington Post*, May 2, 1963.

142 "Production 90, 'Behind the Broken Word' by Roscoe Lee Browne and Anthony Zerbe, March 8–24, 1974," WTCR, box 25, folder 648.

143 "Production 22, 'The Tempest' by William Shakespeare, April 21–May 16, 1965," WTCR, box 3, folders 125–34.

144 Richard L. Coe, "Theater Club's 'The Tempest,'" *Washington Post*, April 29, 1965.
145 Peter Kerr, "Adolph Caesar Dies; Acted in 'Soldier's Story,'" *New York Times*, March 7, 1986.
146 Tom Zito, "The Black Experience," *Washington Post*, August 20, 1970.
147 James Earl Jones and Penelope Niven, *James Earl Jones: Voices and Silences* (New York: Charles Scribner's Sons, 1993), 111–23.
148 Robert Hooks, "Genet's 'The Blacks': Finding the Truths," *Washington Post*, May 27, 1973.
149 Ruble, *Proclaiming Presence*, 211–64.
150 "Production 15, 'The Blacks' by Jean Genet, September 29–October 4, 1964," WTCR, box 3, folders 78–84.
151 "Production 18, 'The Blood Knot' by Artholl Fugard, January 5–21, 1965," WTCR, box 3, folders 100–104.
152 "Production 23, 'Slow Dancing on the Killing Ground,' October 14–November 7, 1965," WTCR, box 4, folders 135–42.
153 R.L.C. [Richard L. Coe], "Theater Club's Debut," *Washington Post*, October 15, 1965.
154 "Slow Dance on the Killing Ground," Plymouth Theater, *Playbill*, November 30, 1964.
155 Richard L. Coe, "Theater Club Opens Tonight," *Washington Post*, October 13, 1965.
156 R.L.C. [Richard L. Coe], "Theater Club's Debut"; Tom Donnelly, "Life and Death and All That Jazz," *Washington Daily News*, October 15, 1965.
157 "Production 40, 'My Sweet Charlie' by David Westheimer, October 12–November 19, 1967," WTCR, box 7, folders 260–68.
158 Bob Todd, "'My Sweet Charlie' Is One Sweet Play," *Washington Daily News*, October 13, 1967.
159 "Production 47, 'The Gingham Dog' by Lanford Wilson, September 26–October 27, 1968," WTCR, box 10, folders 312–17.
160 Lanford Wilson, *The Gingham Dog* (New York: Dramatists Play Service, 1969).
161 Bonnie Aikman, "Theater Club Stages Exciting New Work, *Evening Star*, October 3, 1968; "Seasons of Firsts at WTC," *Washington Post*, August 25, 1968; Richard L. Coe, "WTC Accents the New," *Washington Post*, September 24, 1968; "Marriage on the

Rocks," *Washington Post*, September 28, 1968; Richard L. Coe, "The Gingham Dog: A Fine Production," *Washington Post*, September 28, 1968; Julius Novick, "About Love Gone Sour," *New York Times*, October 13, 1968.

162 "Regional Theater Is Booming," *Hartford Courant*, January 21, 1969; Richard L. Coe, "Dear World, A Swan Song?" *Washington Post*, January 26, 1961; Martin Gottfried, "What Shall It Profit a Theater If . . . ," *New York Times*, August 23, 1970.

163 Jim Laurie, "Theater Club Author Seeks Relevance," *Washington Post*, September 26, 1968.

164 "Production 50, 'Mr. Tambo, Mr. Bones,' by Alexander Panas, January 9–February 9, 1969," WTCR, box 12, folders 332–40.

165 "Program: *Mr. Tambo, Mr. Bones*, January 1969," WTCR, box 12, folder 332.

166 Llewellyn King, "Another Play Within a Play," *Washington Daily News*, January 10, 1969; "A Pair of Premiers," *Washington Post*, January 5, 1969; Geoffrey Wolff, "Play on Booth," *Washington Post*, January 10, 1969.

167 "Production 82, 'Ceremonies in Dark Old Men,' by Lonne Elder III, January 17–February 11; March 6–April 8, 1973)," WTCR, box 23, folders 598–607.

168 "Program: *Ceremonies in Dark Old Men*, March 1973," WTCR, box 23, folder 598.

169 Mel Gussow, "Lonne Elder, 69, Pioneering Playwright, Dies," *New York Times*, June 13, 1996.

170 "New O Street Location for 'Ceremonies,'" *Washington Post*, February 17, 1973.

171 Jeannette Smyth, "Fresh Promise of Success," *Washington Post*, June 20, 1972.

172 "Production 87, 'Inner City,' by Eve Merriam and Hellen Miller, July 18–December 23 and July 11–August 4, 1974," WTCR, box 25, folder 645.

173 "Program: *Inner City*, July 1974," WTCR, box 25, folder 645.

174 Richard L. Coe, "He's Hooked on Universality," *Washington Post*, July 29, 1974.

175 Richard L. Coe, "Theater," *Washington Post*, September 8, 1974.

176 Paul Richard, "All for Art and Artists," *Washington Post*, August 30, 1974.

177 Jacqueline Trescott, "Director Steps Toward a National Black Theater," *Washington Post*, September 18, 2002.
178 Richard L. Coe, "Tax Bite Draws Little Reaction," *Washington Post*, January 16, 1969; Richard L. Coe, "National Absorbs Tax," *Washington Post*, November 27, 1969; Richard L. Coe, "Nonprofit Art Groups Taxed, Too," *Washington Post*, December 4, 1969.
179 John B. Williams, "It's Happening in Real Estate; William H. Jones, "$300 Million Plan for West End Unveiled."
180 Richard L. Coe, "A Taxing Season for the Theater Club," *Washington Post*, September 9, 1972.
181 Coe.
182 Tom Shales, "Washington Theater Club: Curtain Time?" *Washington Post*, June 7, 1974.

Toronto

183 James Kaplan, "Stay Up Late," *New Yorker*, January 16, 1989, 36–60.
184 Nick Mount, *Arrival: The Story of CanLit* (Toronto: Anasi, 2017), 55–60.
185 Mount, 10–11, 301.
186 Mount, 8–9.
187 Mount, 64–69.
188 Paul Litt, *The Muses, The Masses, and the Massey Commission* (Toronto: University of Toronto Press, 1992).
189 Mount, *Arrival*, 96–98.
190 Mount, 98–102.
191 Henry Mietkiewicz and Bob Mackowycz, *Dream Tower: The Life and Legacy of Rochdale College* (Toronto: McGraw-Hill Ryerson, 1988).
192 Mount, *Arrival*, 94–96.
193 Mount, 104, 116–18, 153–56.
194 Mount, 156–61.
195 Margaret Atwood, *Survival: A Thematic Guide to Canadian Literature* (Toronto: House of Anansi Press, 1972).
196 Denis W. Johnston, *Up the Mainstream. The Rise of Toronto's Alternative Theatres* (Toronto: University of Toronto Press, 1991).

197 Julius Novick, "'Ecstasy': The Indian's Agony," *New York Times*, May 13, 1973.
198 Johnston, *Up the Mainstream*, 184.
199 Johnston, 3–27.
200 Johnston, 3–4.
201 Johnston, 28–40.
202 Johnston, 41–49.
203 Johnston, 48–49.
204 Johnston, 64–73.
205 Johnston, 121–22.
206 Johnston, 50–64.
207 Johnston, 123–24.
208 Johnston, 132–35.
209 Johnston, 64–77.
210 Johnston, 77–85.
211 "Creeps," *Canadian Theatre Encyclopedia*, www.canadiantheatre.com/dict.pl?term=Creeps.
212 Johnston, *Up the Mainstream*, 87–89.
213 Johnston, 90–100.
214 "Gass, Ken," *Canadian Theatre Encyclopedia*, www.canadiantheatre.com/dict.pl?term=Gass%2C%20Ken.
215 John Mighton, *A Short History of Night*, rev. ed. (Toronto: Playwrights Canada Press, 2007).
216 Keith Beaty, "Profile: Ken Gass," *Toronto Star*, February 13, 2023.
217 Johnston, *Up the Mainstream*, 141–42.
218 Johnston, 143–45.
219 Johnston, 146–47.
220 Johnston, 147–48.
221 Johnston, 149.
222 Johnston, 154–62.
223 Michel Tremblay, *Birth of a Bookworm*, transl. Sheila Fischman (Vancouver: Talonbooks, 2003).
224 Johnston, *Up the Mainstream*, 154–57.
225 Jane Koustas, "From Gélinas to Carrier: Critical Response to Translated Quebec Theatre in Toronto," *Studies in Canadian Literature* 17, no. 2 (1992): 109–28.
226 Johnston, *Up the Mainstream*, 162–63.

227 Johnston, 166–67.
228 Johnston, 167–69.
229 Jessica Riley, ed., *A Man of Letters: The Selected Dramaturgical Correspondence of Urjo Kareda* (Toronto: Playwrights Canada Press, 2017), 2–3.
230 Riley, *Man of Letters*.
231 See https://tarragontheatre.com/.
232 Johnston, *Up the Mainstream*, 57–59.
233 Johnston, 61–62.
234 Johnston, 61–65.
235 Johnston, 171–72.
236 Johnston, 172–73.
237 Johnston, 172.
238 Johnston, 177.
239 Johnston, 180.
240 Johnston, 182.
241 Johnston, 183.
242 Johnston, 184–85.
243 Johnston, 185.
244 Johnston, 188–90.
245 Johnston, 190–91.
246 Johnston, 194–96.
247 Johnston, 197–236.
248 Robertson Davies, "Introduction to an Anthology of Canadian Plays," in *Happy Alchemy: On the Pleasures of Music and the Theatre*, by Robertson Davies, ed. Jennifer Surridge and Brenda Davies (New York: Viking Press, 1997), 139–43, at 141–42.

Kyiv

249 Roman Adrian Cybriwsky, *Kyiv, Ukraine: The City of Domes and Demons from the Collapse of Socialism to the Mass Uprising* (Amsterdam: Amsterdam University Press, 2014).
250 Olena Brachevskaya, Galina Volosiuk, Olena Malynovs'ka, Yaroslav Pilynskyi, Nancy Popson, and Blair Ruble, *Netradytsiini immihranti u Kievi* (Kyiv: Kennan Kyiv Project, 2003).
251 Mayhill C. Fowler, *Beau Monde on Empire's Edge: State and Stage in Soviet Ukraine* (Toronto: University of Toronto Press, 2017).

252 Brachevskaya et al., *Netradytsiini immihranti*, 42.
253 Irena Makaryk and Viriana Tkacz, *Modernism in Kyiv: Jubilant Experimentation* (Toronto: University of Toronto Press, 2015).
254 Fowler, *Beau Monde*, 119.
255 Fowler, 63–194.
256 Fowler, 148.
257 Milan Kundera, *The Book of Laughter and Forgetting* (New York: HarperCollins, 1994), 218.
258 Roman Adrian Cybriwsky, *Kyiv, Ukraine: The City of Domes and Demons from the Collapse of Socialism to the Mass Uprising* (Amsterdam: Amsterdam University Press, 2014), 61–65.
259 Birgit Beumers and Mark Lipovetsky, *Performing Violence: Literary and Theatrical Experiments of New Russian Drama* (Chicago: University of Chicago Press, 2009).
260 See https://ukrainer.net/harmyder/.
261 F. Joseph Dresen, "Contemporary Ukrainian Theater as Baroque Carnival," Woodrow Wilson Center, Kennan Institute Meeting Reports (May 1, 2001).
262 See www.kurbas.org,ua/centre/html.
263 "Lesia Ukrainka National Academic Drama Theater," Internet Encyclopedia of Ukraine, www.encyclopediaofukraine.com/display.asp?linkpath=pages%5CL%5CE%5CLesiaUkrainkaNationalAcademicDramaTheater.htm.
264 "Драматичний театр імені Івана Франка, Київ," *UA.IGotoWorld.com*.
265 "Kiev Academic Operetta Theatre (Kiev)," WorldWalk.Info, http://worldwalk.info/en/catalog/1367/.
266 See http://newtheatre.kiev.ua.
267 See http://newtheatre.kiev.ua/.
268 See https://dollmen.com.ua/.
269 John Freedman, A *Dictionary of Emotions in a Time of War* (Chapel Hill, NC: Laertes Books, 2023).
270 Author's correspondence with Donald Chung, Amy Sze, and William Wong, September–October 2022.
271 Hanna Veselovska, "Living in the War: The Ukrainian Theatre Since the Russian Invasion," *Critical Stages/Scenes critiques*, issue 26, December 2022.
272 Fowler, *Beau Monde*, 148.

273 Iulia Bentia and Pavlo Shopin, "Ukrainian theater after the full-scale Russian invasion: a new sounding of textbook texts," *Art History of Ukraine (Myststvoznavstvo)*, 2023, issue 23, 61–74.
274 See www.ukraine-fringe.com/.

Nashville

275 Ross Laird and Brian Rush, *Discography of OKeh Records, 1918–1934* (Westport, CT: Greenwood, 2004).
276 Dayton Duncan and Ken Burns, *Country Music. An Illustrated History* (New York: Alfred A. Knopf, 2019), 5–7.
277 Ken Emerson, *Doo-dah! Steven Foster and the Rise of American Popular Culture* (New York: Simon & Schuster, 1997).
278 Freddi Williams Evans, *Congo Square: African Roots in New Orleans* (Lafayette: University of Louisiana at Lafayette Press, 2010), 43–45.
279 Duncan and Burns, *Country Music*, 28–29.
280 Duncan and Burns, 19–28.
281 Duncan and Burns, 20.
282 Michael Kosser, *How Nashville Became Music City USA: A History of Music Row*, 2nd edition (Essex, CT: Backbeat Books, 2022), 1–4.
283 Duncan and Burns, *Country Music*, 92–99.
284 William U. Eiland, *Nashville's Mother Church: The History of the Ryman Auditorium* (Nashville: Abe Books, 1992).
285 Duncan and Burns, *Country Music*, 66–69.
286 Duncan and Burns, 71–79.
287 Kosser, *How Nashville Became Music City USA*, p. 2.
288 Duncan and Burns, *Country Music*, pp. 92-99.
289 Eiland, *Nashville's Mother Church*.
290 Duncan and Burns, *Country Music*, p. 109.
291 Kosser, *How Nashville Became Music City USA*, 1.
292 Campbell Gibson, "Population of the 100 Largest Cities and Other Urban Places in the United States: 1790 to 1990," US Census working paper, 1998, www.census.gov/library/working-papers/1998/demo/POP-twps0027.html.
293 See www.countrymusichalloffame.org/about/collections/oral-history/david-cobb-3.

Notes

294 Kosser, *How Nashville Became Music City USA*, 3–18.
295 Kosser, 1.
296 Kosser, xii.
297 Duncan and Burns, *Country Music*, 209–13.
298 Kosser, *How Nashville Became Music City USA*, 19–26.
299 Duncan and Burns, *Country Music*, 209–13.
300 Duncan and Burns, 23.
301 Kosser, *How Nashville Became Music City USA*, 107.
302 Kosser, 259.
303 James Miller, *Flowers in the Dustbin: The Rise of Rock and Roll, 1947–1977* (New York: Simon & Shuster, 1999).
304 Duncan and Burns, *Country Music*, 225–30.
305 Duncan and Burns, 377–80.
306 Kosser, *How Nashville Became Music City USA*, 51–55.
307 Kosser, 53.
308 Duncan and Burns, *Country Music*, 230–33.
309 Kosser, *How Nashville Became Music City USA*, 41–42.
310 Duncan and Burns, *Country Music*, 243–44,
311 Duncan and Burns, 220.
312 Duncan and Burns, 322–23.
313 Duncan and Burns, 273.
314 Duncan and Burns, 351–66.
315 Duncan and Burns.
316 Eiland, *Nashville's Mother Church*.
317 Leena Konar, "10 Reasons Why You Should Visit Nashville," Culture Trip website, May 2, 2017, https://theculturetrip.com/northamerica/usa/tennessee/articles/10-reasons-why-you-should-visit-nashville.

Concluding Observations

318 See, for example, https://www.arts.gov/impact/research/arts-data-profile-series/adp-33; and, https://www.americansforthearts.org/sites/default/files/pdf/information_services/research/services/economic_impact/aepiv/DC_GreaterWashingtonMetroRegion_SampleReport.pdf.
319 https://torontoartscouncil.org/TAC/media/tac/Advocacy/Toronto-Arts-Facts.pdf.

320 As discussed in Iro Valaskakis Tembeck, "Politics and Dance in Montreal, 1940s to 1980s: The Imaginary Maginot Line between Anglophone and Francophone Dancers," in *Canadian Dance: Visions and Stories*, ed. Selma Landen Odom and Mary Jane Warner (Toronto: Dance Collection Danse Press, 2004), pp.78-280; and, Iro Tembeck, *Dancing in Montreal: Seeds of a Choreographic History* (Oak Creek, WI: Society of Dance History Scholars, 1994).

321 For further discussion of this point, see Blair A. Ruble, *Proclaiming Presence from the Washington Stage* (Washington, D.C.: New Academia Publishing, Inc., 2021).

322 As discussed in Iulia Bentia and Pavlo Shopin, "Ukrainian theater after the full-scale Russian invasion: a new sounding of textbook texts," *Art History of Ukraine (Myststvoznavstvo)*, 2023, issue 23, 61–74.

Index

Academic Theater of Russian Drama (Kyiv), 81
Académie Française, 2, 3
activism, 9, 39–40, 42, 47, 49
Actors' Equity Guild, 9, 42, 64
Acuff, Roy, 104, 108, 113
Adu, Frank, 48
African Americans: Jim Crow policies, 37, 39, 41–43; as majority population of Washington, DC, 8; "race music" promoted to, 99, 100; as theater/writers/artists, 9, 39, 41–48, 51
Allen, Paul, 48–49
All Souls Unitarian Church (Washington, DC), 39–40, 42
alternative theater, 11, 58, 59, 66–71, 96
Altman, Robert: *Nashville*, 112
American Ballet Theatre (New York), 21, 24
Angelou, Maya, 45
Anthony, Mary, 27
Arena Stage (Washington, DC), 42, 50
Armstrong, Louis, 100
Arnoult, Philip, 90
artistic change, relationship with urban change, 4–6, 16, 49, 59, 71–73, 87, 114–16
Astaseva, Olena: *A Dictionary of Emotions in a Time of War*, 90
Atkins, Chet, 111
Atwood, Margaret, 54, 57–58
authoritarianism, 5, 80, 82, 93

Les Automatistes, 17, 18, 26
Autry, Gene, 104
avant-garde dance, 29, 34
avant-garde theater, 84

Baby Boom generation, 55, 116
Bailey, DeFord, 15, 101
Baker, Peggy, 33
Balanchine, George, 22
ballet, 7, 19–34, 53
Le Ballet Jazz de Montrèal, 26, 30–31, 34
Les Ballets Chiriaeff, 20, 23, 30
Les Ballets-Québec, 20
Les Ballets Russes, 7, 19, 20
Banneker, Benjamin, 8
Bates, Humphrey, 101
Beatty, Ned, 39
Beaudet, Marc, 19
Beiderbecke, Bix, 100
Belinsky, Sacha, 26
Beliveau, Bernadette, 22
Bentia, Iulia, 93, 94
Berezil', 79, 80, 85
Bergman, Ingrid, 41–42
Bergonier, Auguste, 84
Berlin: dance scene, 20, 22, 23; hipster art districts, 75; theater scene, 79
Bess, Hattie Louise "Tootsie," 109–10
Bettis, Paul, 63
Bevington, Stan, 57
Birksted-Breen, Noah, 90
Bissonnette, Lise, 57
Black American Theater (Washington, DC), 48

Black community. *See* African Americans
Black Repertory Company (Washington, DC), 45
Black Spectrum Theatre Company of Queens (New York), 48
Black theater/writers/artists, 9, 39, 41–48, 51
Blais, Marie-Clair, 57
Bloom, Alan, 53
blues music, 100, 105, 109
Boas, Franziska, 18
Bolt, Carol, 70, 71
Bomers, Bernie, 66
Boneham, Peter, 27–28, 33
Bongard, Madeleine, 95
Borduas, Paul-Émile, 18
Born, Max, 10
Borovenskiy, Alex, 94–96
Bosy, Pavlo, 83
Boudot, Michel, 19
Bourgogne Theater (Kyiv), 84
Bowering, George, 57
bpNichol, 57
Bradley, Harold, 107, 108
Bradley, Owen, 107, 108, 111
Brazwell, Damon, 41, 46
Brecht, Berthold, 44
Broderick, James, 39
Bron, Eleanor, 39
Browne, Roscoe Lee, 39, 44, 45
Buckle, Richard, 23
Byrd, Charlie, 39–40
Caesar, Adolph, 39, 44, 45
Cambridge, Edmund, 45
Cambridge, Godfrey, 45
Camus, Albert: *Caligula*, 41, 93–94
Canada: arts defining identity of, 59; dance culture, 19; French-Canadian identity, 19, 21, 26, 29; labor shortages, 35; literary canon of, 54–58; literary identity, 58–59; national identity, development of, 11, 21, 24, 53, 58, 59, 63, 71; radio and television, 7, 18–20, 24, 30, 35, 117; university system expansion, 55; World War II refugees, 22. *See also specific cities and provinces*
Canadian Place Theatre, 69
Canadian Rep Theatre, 64, 65
Canadian Stage Company, 68, 71
Capson, Louis: *I Love You Billy Striker*, 64
Carson, Fiddlin' John, 100
Carter, Jimmy, 112
Carter family (music group), 101, 104
Cash, Johnny, 111
Castle, Irene and Vernon, 19
Catherine II (empress of Russia), 12
Catholicism, 6, 9–10, 21, 42, 77
Catlett, Mary Jo, 39
Caton, Edward, 22
Cavallari, Ivan, 25
censorship, 2–3, 77
Central Library Theater (Toronto), 61
CentreStage (Toronto), 68, 71
Charles, Ray, 111
Charles X (king of France), 1–4
Chernobyl nuclear accident (1986), 13
children's theater, 38, 62, 93
Chiriaeff, Alexis, 20
Chiriaeff, Ludmilla, 20–25, 30, 31, 34
choreography, 20, 21, 24–29, 32–34
Choromanski, Michel, 21
Christie Pits Riots (Toronto, 1933), 10–11
Christy, Edwin Pearce, 101
Chung, Donald, 91
circus arts, 33
Civil Rights Act of 1964, 45
Clark, Bryan, 47

144   Index

classical dance, 7, 17, 21, 23, 33, 34
Classicists, 1–4
CMA (Country Music Association), 110–12
Coach House Press, 56–57
Cobb, David, 107, 110
Coe, Richard L., 43, 44
Cohen, Leonard, 54, 56
Cohen, Nathan, 59
Comédie Française, 2–4
Communist Party, 13, 79, 80, 84
contemporary dance, 26–33
Cote, Marie, 22
Counterculturalists, 2
country music: commercialization of, 16, 96–97, 99–101; Countrypolitan sound, 110–12; *The Grand Ole Opry* radio program and, 15–16, 102–5, 107, 112–13; Honky Tonk Row and, 110, 113; Music Row and, 106–9, 111; Opryland entertainment complex and, 16, 103, 113, 114; rebranding efforts, 110–12; Ryman Auditorium and, 16, 103, 105, 112, 113; urban development impacted by, 16, 114, 115
Country Music Association (CMA), 110–12
Country Music Hall of Fame (Nashville), 111, 113
COVID-19 pandemic, 65, 68, 88, 114, 117, 118
Craig, Edwin, 15, 16, 102–4
Craske, Margaret, 22
Creation 2 (Toronto), 71
Crevier, Gérald, 17, 19–23, 34
Crimea, Russian annexation of (2014), 76, 87, 89
Cunningham, Merce, 27, 29
Cybriwsky, Roman, 75, 76

dance: avant-garde, 29, 34; ballet, 7, 19–34, 53; choreography and, 20, 21, 24–29, 32–34; circus arts and, 33; classical, 7, 17, 21, 23, 33, 34; contemporary, 26–33; diversification within, 23, 28, 31–33; experimental, 26, 34; identity and, 19, 21, 26, 29, 31–32; modern, 7, 18, 21–22, 26–27, 33–34, 37, 78; performance, 5–7, 17, 20, 23, 32–35, 115–17; physical theater and, 33; politics and, 26, 31, 33, 35; ritualistic traditions, 32
Danchenko, Serhiy, 85
Danse-Cité, 29, 32
Darnell, Robert, 47
Davies, Robertson, 71–72
Denisova, Sasha, 82, 88
Denning, J. Gordon, 22
Devaux, Elisabeth "Zette," 20
Diaghilev, Sergei, 19, 26
digital media, 117–18
Dixie Tabernacle (Nashville), 16, 103–5
documentary theater, 88
Dodson, Owen, 42
DollMen Theater Company (Kyiv), 88–89
Donelson, John, 14
drama. *See* theater
Dramatists' Guild, 42
Drapeau, Jean, 25
Dudek, Louis, 56
Dukakis, Olympia, 65
Dumont, Gabriel, 70
Duncan, Isadora, 7
Dunham, Katherine, 43
Duplessis, Maurice, 6
Duras, Marguerite, 95
Dwyer, Peter, 23

Ebony Promptu Theater Company (Washington, DC), 48
Einstein, Albert, 10
Elder, Lonne, III: *Ceremonies in Dark Old Men*, 47–48
electronic media, 117
Époque, Martine, 28
equestrian theater, 83
Euromaidan (Ukraine, 2013–14), 75, 86
Exit/In club (Nashville), 110
experimental dance, 26, 34
experimental theater, 9, 37–51, 60, 78, 82, 93, 95

Factory Theatre Lab (Toronto), 59, 63–66
Faierstein, Roslyn, 26
Faison, George, 48–49
La famille Plouffe (television series), 18
Farrell, James T., 43
Fichandler, Zelda and Thomas, 42, 50
Flack, Roberta, 42
Fleisher, Leon, 38
Fokine, Michel, 20
folk music, 42, 56, 100, 105, 111
Ford, Henry, 101
Fortier, Paul-André, 28–29, 33
Fortune, John, 39
Foster, Stephen, 100–101
Fowler, Mayhill C., 77, 78, 80, 92
France: censorship, 2–3; Classicists vs. Romanticists, 1–4; generational change, 1–2; July Revolution in (1830), 4; Old Regime of, 1, 2, 4. *See also* Paris
Frankel, Gene, 45
Freedman, John, 90
Freeman, David: *Creeps*, 63–66
French-Canadian identity, 19, 21, 26, 29

Frye, Northrop, 53, 57
Fugard, Atholl: *The Blood Knot*, 45

Gagnier, Lise, 20
Gallant, Mavis, 54
Garland, Hank, 108
GaRmYdEr (Garmyder) theater (Lutsk, Ukraine), 82–83
Garrard, Jim, 60, 61, 69
Gass, Ken, 63–65
Gélinas, Marc, 71
generational change, 1–2, 16, 96
Genet, Jean: *The Blacks: A Clown Show*, 44–45
Gerroll, Daniel, 95
Getz, Stan, 39–40
Gielgud, John, 42
Glassco, Bill, 63, 65–68, 71
Glassco, Jane, 65, 66
Global Village Theater (Toronto), 67, 71
Godfrey, Dave, 57
Goldman, Emma, 71
Goldstein, William: *Mr. Tambo, Mr. Bones*, 47
Gordone, Charles, 39, 45
gospel music, 100, 111
Gossett, Louis, Jr., 45
Gould, Glenn, 54
Gove, Steve, 94
Graham, Martha, 18, 22
The Grand Ole Opry (radio program), 15–16, 102–5, 107, 112–13
Les Grands Ballets Canadiens, 21–30, 32–34
Grant, Micki, 39, 44, 47
Great Famine (1930–33), 80
Gremina, Elena, 88
Le Groupe de la Place Royale, 26–29, 31

Le Groupe Nouvelle Aire, 26, 28–29, 31–33
Gunn, Bill, 39, 43

Hackman, Gene, 39
Hamilton, Alexander, 7
Hanley, William: *Slow Dance on a Killing Ground*, 46
Harman, Buddy, 108
Hart House Theatre (Toronto), 70
Hartke, Gilbert V., 42
Hatcher, Jeffrey, 95
Hay, George D., 15
Hébert, Anne, 57
Heinemann, Otto K. E., 100, 101
Hemenway, Nora, 29
Hendry, Tom, 61, 68–70
Herbert, John, 63
hillbilly music. *See* country music
Hillerman, John, 39, 41, 46, 47
Hillsboro Theatre (Nashville), 16, 103, 104
hip-hop, 87
Holm, Hanya, 22, 27
Honky Tonk Row (Nashville), 110, 113
Hooks, Robert, 45
Horne, Geoffrey, 43
Horst, Louis, 18
House of Anansi Press, 57–58
housing segregation, 8
Howard, Bette, 48
Hübl, Milan, 80–81
Hugo, Victor: *Hernani, ou l'Honneur Castillan*, 3–4; *The Last Day of a Condemned Man*, 2; *Marion de Larme* (*Un Duel sous Richelieu*), 2–3
Humphrey, Doris, 22
Hyman, Earl, 42

identity: Canadian national, 11, 21, 24, 53, 58, 59, 63, 71; dance and, 19, 21, 26, 29, 31–32; emotional mobilization and, 117; French-Canadian, 19, 21, 26, 29; literary, 58–59; of Ryman Auditorium, 105; secularization and loosening of, 6; Ukrainian, 76
immigrants: folk music and, 100; in Montreal, 7, 18–22, 31, 35; in Toronto, 9–11, 56, 59, 72, 116; in Ukraine, 76
improvisational theater, 60–62, 72
Infeld, Leopold, 10
inventive theater. *See* experimental theater
Ionescu, Eugen: *The Lesson*, 37
Ivan Franko Theater (Kyiv), 80, 84, 85, 93

Jackson, Daniel, 28, 33
Jacobs, Jane, 54
jazz ballet, 26, 30–31, 34
jazz music, 39–40, 42, 54, 56, 99–101, 110, 111
Jefferson, Thomas, 7
Jews: Ford's anti-semitism, 101; Kyiv and Ukraine, 12, 77–80; Toronto, 10–11
Jim Crow policies, 37, 39, 41–43
Johnson, Sheila, 48
Johnston, Denis W., 58, 59, 66, 69, 70
Johnstone, Kenneth, 22
Jones, Betty, 32
Jones, James Earl, 45
joual dialect, 66
July Revolution (France, 1830), 4

Kaminska, Esther Kokhl, 78
Kaplan, James, 53

Kareda, Urjo, 59, 67–68, 70, 72
Kass, Peter, 65
Kennedy Center (New York), 38, 45
Kerr, Walter: *Sing Out, Sweet Land*, 42
Kharkiv: as capital of Soviet Ukraine, 12, 78–79; theater scene, 79, 80, 85, 87, 89
Kinal, Sylvia, 26
Kinch, Martin, 61, 68–70
King, Martin Luther, Jr., 47
King, Philip: *See How They Run*, 40
Kirstein, Lincoln, 23–24
Klein, A. M., 56
Kniaseff, Boris, 22
Kollar, Leena, 114
Kosodiy, Anastasia, 89
Kosser, Michael, 104, 106–11
Kostiumynskyi, Dmytro, 88–89
Koston, Dina, 38
Kotto, Yaphet, 39, 45
Kryzhanovsky, Alexander, 86
Kudelka, James, 33
Kundera, Milan: *The Book of Laughter and Forgetting*, 80–81
Kurbas, Les', 78–81, 83, 85
Kurochkin, Maksym, 82, 87, 88, 90–91
Kyiv: dance scene, 23, 78; Fringe Festival in (2023), 94–96; hipster art districts, 75; population growth, 12, 13, 76; Soviet government, 12–13, 79; status as international capital, 13, 75, 117; theater scene, 5, 77–96, 115, 116

Lacasse, Adelard, 19
Lacasse, Maurice. *See* Morenoff, Maurice
La La La Human Steps, 29, 32
La Mama Experimental Theatre Club (New York), 60
Lambert, Marjorie, 29
Larner, Jeremy, 48
La Tour, Nick, 45
Laurin, Ginette, 28, 29
Lawless, Sue, 46
Lèbe, Rose-Marie, 28
Lecavalier, Louise, 28, 32
Lee, Dennis, 57
Leese, Elizabeth, 21–24
Legat, Nicolas, 22
Lemelin, Roger, 18
L'Enfant, Pierre, 7–8
Leningrad. *See* St. Petersburg
Lennon, Jon: *In His Own Words*, 61
Lepage, Roland, 67
Lesage, Jean, 6
Lesya Ukrainka Theater (Kyiv), 84
Léveillé, Daniel, 28, 29
Limón, José, 32
Lincoln, Abraham, 8, 47
Little Globe Theater (Kirovohrad, Ukraine), 83
Lock, Édouard, 28, 29, 32
Loe, Erlend, 95
London: dance scene, 23, 27; hipster art districts in, 75; theater scene, 58, 60
Lorrain, Roland, 19
Loubert, Candace, 32
Louis-Philippe I (king of France), 4

MacDonald, Anne-Marie, 57
MacDonald, Brian, 22, 25
MacEwen, Gwendolyn, 57
Macon, Dave, 101
Madison, James, 7
Mangum, Edward, 42
Manier, Owsley, 110
Marlin-Jones, Davey, 37–38, 43, 46, 47, 51
Marshall, Dora, 20
Martin, Grady, 108

Massey, Raymond, 55
Massey, Vincent and Massey Commission, 55
Mayakovsky Theater (Moscow), 88
McLuhan, Marshall, 53
McNally, Terrence: *Sweet Eros*, 61
Merriam, Eve: *Inner City*, 48
Merrick, David, 43
Michaels, Anne, 57
Mighton, John: *A Short History of Night*, 64–65
Mikhoels, Solomon, 80
Millaire, Andrée, 20
Miller, Helen: *Inner City*, 48
minstrel shows, 47, 101
Miranda, Lin-Manuel: *Hamilton*, 7
Mirolla, Michael: *Snails*, 63
modern dance, 7, 18, 21–22, 26–27, 33–34, 37, 78
Monette, Richard, 67
Monroe, Bill, 104
Montana, Patsy, 104
Montreal: dance scene, 5–7, 17, 19–35, 115–17; Expo '67 World's Fair, 24, 25, 70; immigrants, 7, 18–22, 31, 35; linguistic divide, 7, 35, 116; literary scene, 56; politics, 23, 26, 31, 33, 35; radio and television, 7, 18, 20, 35, 117; theater scene, 25, 61, 66, 69
Montréal Danse, 28, 29, 33
Montreal Theatre Ballet, 22
Moore, Bob, 108
morality, 61, 62, 70–71, 82, 93–95
Morenoff, Carmen, 19, 21–23, 26
Morenoff, Maurice, 19, 21–24, 26
Morris, Margaret, 22
Moscow: dance scene, 23; theater scene, 77, 79, 82
Mostel, Joshua, 39
Munro, Alice, 54

music: blues, 100, 105, 109; chamber music ensembles, 38; choreography independent of, 27; folk, 42, 56, 100, 105, 111; gospel, 100, 111; hip-hop, 87; jazz, 39–40, 42, 54, 56, 99–101, 110, 111; radio stations and, 15–16, 99, 102–5. *See also* country music
Music Row (Nashville), 106–9, 111
Napoleon Bonaparte, 1, 2
Nash, Francis, 14
Nashville: establishment of, 14; as "Music City," 102, 106–10, 117; Parthenon replica in, 14; population growth, 14, 15, 106; suburbanization, 106; urban transformation of, 5, 15, 103, 105–7, 113–16. *See also* country music
National Academic Operetta Theater (Kyiv), 85–86
National Ballet of Canada, 20, 21, 23
nationalism, 6, 12–13, 23–26, 31, 54–59, 63, 71
National Theater (Washington, DC), 42, 50
Nault, Fernand, 19, 21, 24, 25, 29
Negro Ensemble Company (New York), 45, 47
Nejdana, Neda, 88, 95
Newman, William T., Jr., 48
New Russian Drama movement, 82, 87
New Theatre (Toronto), 71
New Vic Theatre (Toronto), 69
New York City: dance scene, 18, 20–21, 23–24, 27; hipster art districts, 75; as mecca of creativity, 53; theater scene, 41, 43–48, 58, 60, 63
Nijinska, Bronislawa, 78

Nikolaeva, Alexandra, 22
Nixon, Richard, 113
Novick, Julius, 58

Odom, Selma Landen, 26
Oermann, Robert, 109
O'Horigan, Tom, 48
OKeh music label, 15, 100
Oliver, King, 100
Olney Summer Theater (Maryland), 42
Ondaatje, Michael, 55, 57, 70
Ontario: budgetary issues, 72; culture sector and GDP of, 116; dance scene, 28, 31. *See also* Toronto
Open Circle (Toronto), 71
Opryland entertainment complex (Nashville), 16, 103, 113, 114
Orange Revolution (Ukraine, 2004–5), 86
Orchid Lounge (Nashville), 109–10
Otzup-Gorny, Ludmilla. *See* Chiriaeff, Ludmilla
Owens, Rochelle: *Futz*, 60–61

Page, P. K., 56
Pale of Settlement, 77, 78
Palmer, John, 61, 68–69
Panas, Alexander: *Mr. Tambo, Mr. Bones*, 47
Pankov, Gradimir, 25
Paris: dance scene, 21–23, 27; generational divisions, 1; hipster art districts, 75; theater culture, 2–4
patriotism. *See* nationalism
Pavlova, Anna, 7, 20
Payette, Mike, 68
Pearl, Minnie, 104
Peer, Ralph, 99–101
Pereyaslav, Treaty of (1654), 12
performance dance, 5–7, 17, 20, 23, 32–35, 115–17
performing arts: as communal experiences, 118; digital media's impact on, 117–18; economic impact of, 116; financial support for, 117; nationalism and, 23, 26; relationship between urban and artistic change in, 4–6, 16, 49, 59, 71–73, 87, 114–15; taxes imposed on admission to events, 50. *See also* dance; music; theater
Perreault, Jean-Pierre, 27, 32
Perron, Maurice, 18
Pfoutz, Shirley: *The Whipping Boy*, 43
Phillips, Sam, 109
Phoenix Theatre (Toronto), 71
physical theater, 33, 88
Polish theater, 78
Poltava Puppet Theater, 93
Porytski, Ruslana and Pavlo, 82–83
Protestantism, 6, 9–11, 62, 77
puppet theater, 38, 70, 88, 89, 93

Quebec: clerical power, 6, 17, 18, 23, 33; culture wars, 17, 33; dance scene, 5–7, 18–35; economy of, 6, 17, 18; French-Canadian identity, 19, 21, 26, 29; modernization of, 6, 18, 31, 33, 35; nationalism in, 6, 23, 24, 26, 31, 54; politics in, 18, 23–26, 31–33, 35; Quiet Revolution, 5, 6, 24–25, 31; secularization of, 5, 6, 24, 31; separatism/sovereignty movement, 6, 29, 31–32, 35, 51, 54, 66, 72, 116. *See also* Montreal

Québécois identity. *See* French-Canadian identity
Quiet Revolution (Quebec), 5, 6, 24–25, 31

Rabin, Linda, 32, 33
race: Ford's racism, 101; housing segregation based on, 8; integration and racial clashes, 39, 42–44, 106; Jim Crow policies, 37, 39, 41–43; music promotion based on, 99, 100; theater's engagement with race relations, 42–48; white supremacist ideology, 14. *See also* African Americans
Ramsey, Logan, 44
Rawlins, Lester, 39, 44
Red Barn Theatre (Jackson's Pass, Ontario), 65
Le Refus Global (artistic manifesto), 17, 27, 34
religion. *See specific religions*
Renaud, Jeanne, 26–27, 33
Revolution of Dignity. *See* Euromaidan
Reynolds, Brugh, 110
Reznikovych, Mykhailo Yuriiovych, 84
Rhodes, Lawrence, 25
Richler, Mordecai, 55, 56
Riel, Louis, 70
Riley, Jessica, 68
Riopelle, Françoise, 27
Riopelle, Jean-Paul, 18
Ritter, Tex, 104
Robertson, Eck, 100
Robertson, James, 14
Rochdale College (Toronto), 56–58, 60, 63, 65, 66, 69
Rodgers, Jimmy, 101, 111
Romanticists, 1–4

Rose, Fred, 108, 111
Rose, Richard, 68
Royal Winnipeg Ballet, 21, 23, 30
Ruban, Viktor, 89
Rushkovsky, Nikolay, 86
Russia: censorship, 77; Crimea annexation (2014), 76, 87, 89; music scene, 78, 79; New Russian Drama movement, 82, 87; political upheaval, 12, 78; television, 82, 88; theater scene, 77–79, 82, 87–88; Ukraine invasion (2022), 84, 89–94. *See also* Soviet Union; *specific cities*
Russian Orthodox Church, 12, 82
Ruvenoff, Ezzak, 20
Ryman Auditorium (Nashville), 16, 103, 105, 112, 113

St. Denis, Ruth, 7
St. Jacques, Raymond, 45
St.-Laurent, Louis, 55
St. Petersburg: dance scene, 21, 23; imperial powers in, 12; theater scene, 77, 79
Salbaing, Geneviève, 30, 31
Salzburg Landes Theatre, 30
Saunders, Leslie Howard, 10
Scott, F. R., 56
Scott, Len, 45
secularization, 5, 6, 24, 31
segregated housing, 8
Semdor-Doroshenko, Semen, 78
Shakespeare, William, 44, 65, 69, 85, 88
Shevchenko, Taras, 93, 94
Shevchenko Theater (Kharkiv), 80
Sholes, Steve, 108
Shopin, Pavlo, 93, 94
Shurtleff, Michael: *Call Me By My Rightful Name*, 43

Shyshko, Kost, 83
Sierra, Carmen. *See* Morenoff, Carmen
Simcoe, John Graves, 9–10
slavery and enslaved persons, 8, 100, 101
Smith, A. J. M., 56
Smith, Mamie, 100
Smith, William Crawford, 14
social media, 87, 117, 118
Söderberg, Hjalmar, 95
Sokolow, Anna, 32
Solovtsov Theater (Kyiv), 85
Sophocles: *Oedipus Rex*, 93, 94
Sorel, Ruth, 21–23
Sorrell, W. Byron, 50
Soulières, Daniel, 32–33
Soviet Union: collapse of, 81, 116; First Five-Year-Plan era (1928–32), 80; Great Famine (1930–33), 80; Ukraine as member of, 12–13, 78–81, 84–85. *See also* Russia; *specific cities*
Spencer, Bob, 47
Stalin, Joseph, 80
Stearns, Linda, 25, 27
Stener, Eric, 63
Studio Lab Theatre (Toronto), 71
Sullivan, Françoise, 17–18, 20, 22–23, 33, 34
Sutton, Dolores, 44
Suzuki, David, 54
Sze, Amy, 91

Tabort, George, 44
Tarragon Theatre (Toronto), 59, 66–68, 72
Teekman, Tassy, 33
Tembeck, Iro Valaskakis, 25–26, 31
theater: activism and, 9, 39–40, 42, 49; alternative, 11, 58, 59, 66–71, 96; avant-garde, 84; children's, 38, 62, 93; claiming presence through, 37, 51; Classicist vs. Romanticist, 2–4; COVID-19 pandemic and, 65, 68, 88; documentary, 88; engagement with race relations, 42–48; equestrian, 83; experimental, 9, 37–51, 60, 78, 82, 93, 95; grassroots movements, 63, 115; improvisational, 60–62, 72; minstrel shows, 47, 101; morality and, 61, 62, 70–71, 82, 93–95; physical, 33, 88; puppet, 38, 70, 88, 89, 93; Quiet Revolution and, 25; as safe space during wartime, 93–96; urban change and effects on, 5, 49, 59, 71–73, 87; variety shows, 19, 79, 101
Theater of Luminaries (Teatr Koryfiev, Ukrainian-language theater), 78
Theater of Playwrights (Kyiv), 88, 90
Theater on Pechersk (Kyiv), 86
Theater on Podil (Kyiv), 93
Theatre d'Audjourd'hui (Montreal), 61
Theatre Passe Muraille (Toronto), 57, 59–63, 68, 69
Thompson, Paul, 61–62
Thompson, "Uncle Jimmy," 15
Todd, Bob, 46
Toronto: Christie Pits Riots (1933), 10–11; dance scene, 20, 22; deindustrialization, 59; gentrification, 72; identity developed by, 11; immigrants, 9–11, 56, 59, 72, 116; literary scene, 55–58; music scene, 54, 56; nationalism in,

54, 58–59, 63, 71; radio and television, 18; theater scene, 5, 11, 51, 58–73, 115, 117; urban transformation of, 9, 11, 71–73, 115–16
Toronto Free Theatre, 57, 59, 61, 68–71
Toussaint, Eddy, 30–31
Treaty of Pereyaslav (1654), 12
Tremblay, Michel, 55, 66–67
Trotz, Frank, 63
Troyanoff, V. G., 30
Trudeau, Margaret, 62
Trudeau, Pierre Elliott, 54, 62
Tse, Tomas K. H., 95
Tubb, Ernest, 105
Tudor, Antony, 22
Tyson, Cicely, 45

Ugarov, Mikhail, 88
Ukraine: change from Russian to Ukrainian identity, 76; Chernobyl nuclear accident (1986), 13; Euromaidan (2013–14), 75, 86; as founding member of United Nations, 13; immigrants, 76; independence of, 5, 13, 80–82, 84, 87, 96, 115; music scene, 81, 87; nationalism in, 12–13; Orange Revolution (2004–5), 86; Russian annexation of Crimea (2014), 76, 87, 89; Russian invasion of (2022), 84, 89–94; Soviet Union and, 12–13, 78–81, 84–85; theater scene, 5, 77–96, 115, 116. *See also specific cities*
Ukraine Fringe Festival, 94–96
Ukrainian Odyssey project, 88–90
Ukrainka, Lesya: *Cassandra*, 93, 94
Unitarian Players, 37, 39, 40, 49

United Nations, 13
United States: bureaucratic expansion in, 8, 49; Counterculturalists in, 2; cultural imperialism of, 54; postwar economy of, 11; radio and television, 15–16, 18, 99, 102–5. *See also specific cities*
urban change, relationship with artistic change, 4–6, 16, 49, 59, 71–73, 87, 114–16

Vaillancourt, Pauline, 27
Vallièrès, Pierre, 71
Van Burek, John, 67
variety shows, 19, 79, 101
Veselovska, Hanna, 92
Vofozhbit, Natal'ya, 82
Volkoff, Boris, 22
von Gencsy, Eva, 30–31
Voronova, Madame, 29
Vorozhbut, Natalka, 87–89, 91

Walker, George F., 63
Walter, Bruno, 21
Wanamaker, Sam, 41–42
War Memorial Auditorium (Nashville), 16, 103, 105
Warner, Mary Jane, 26
Washington, DC: African Americans as majority population of, 8; Compromise of 1970 and, 7; congressional control of, 5, 8, 9, 50; economic impact of performing arts, 116; home rule for, 5, 8, 9, 50; Jim Crow policies, 37, 39, 41–43; origins and growth of, 7–9; theater scene, 5, 9, 37–51, 115, 117
Washington, George, 7
Washington Theater Club, 37–51;

Black theater and artists promoted by, 9, 39, 41–48, 51; educational outreach activities, 38, 41, 50; engagement with race relations, 42–48; financial issues, 9, 38, 40, 41, 48–50; origins and expansion of, 37–41; as proving ground for actors, 9, 39
Waugh, Irving, 113
Weidman, Charles, 7
Wentworth, Hazel, 37–46, 48–51
Wentworth, John B., 37, 39–46, 49–51
Westheimer, David: *My Sweet Charlie*, 46
white supremacist ideology, 14
Whittaker, Herbert, 59, 72
Wigman, Mary, 7
Wilcox, Collin, 43
Williams, Billy Dee, 39, 45, 46
Williams, Hank, 108, 111
Willis, Bob, 104
Wilson, Lanford: *The Gingham Dog*, 46–47
Wong, William, 91
Worldwide Ukrainian Play Readings Project, 90–92
WSM (radio station), 15–16, 102–5, 107, 112, 113
Wysocka, Stanisława, 78

Yanukovych, Viktor, 75
Yiddish theater, 78, 79

Zaré, Séda, 21–23, 30
Zerbe, Anthony, 44
Zimmerman, Ralph, 63

How the Performing Arts Paradoxically Transform
Conflict-Ridden Cities into Centers of
Cultural Innovation

*"These essays, woven together in an imaginative
and creative fashion, are quite wonderful."*
—*Joseh S. Tulchin, Senior Scholar, Woodrow Wilson Center*

A Trilogy

The Muse of Urban Delirium
Proclaiming Presence from the Washington Stage
Changing Cities, Shifting Stages

How in Washington DC, theater offered a path to recognition for African Americans, Roman Catholic clerics, and community activists.

"Blair Ruble has done what no one else up to this point has, constructed a comprehensive critical analysis of Washington DC's theater scene."
—Derek Hyra, Founding Director, Metropolitan Policy Center, American University

Order from: www.amazon.com
www.bn.com
www.newacademia.com

www.ingramcontent.com/pod-product-compliance
Lightning Source LLC
Chambersburg PA
CBHW051106160426
43193CB00010B/1337